EXTRAORDINARY
WOMEN SCIENTISTS

EXTRAORDINARY WOMEN SCIENTISTS

By Darlene R. Stille

Consultants

Angela V. Olinto, Ph. D.,
Senior Lecturer,
Department of Astronomy and Astrophysics,
University of Chicago

Enid Schildkrout, Ph. D.,
Curator, American Museum of Natural History and
Professor of Anthropology,
Columbia University

Lucy Shapiro, Ph. D.,
Joseph D. Grant Professor in the School of Medicine and
Chairman, Department of Developmental Biology,
Stanford University Medical Center, Stanford, California

CHILDRENS PRESS®
CHICAGO

Project editor: Flanagan Publishing Services

Designer and electronic page composition: Lindaanne Donohoe Design

Photo researcher: Feldman & Associates, Inc.

Copy editor: Irene Keller

Indexer: Schroeder Indexing Services

Engraver: RT Associates, Inc.

Printer: Lake Book Manufacturing, Inc.

**Library of Congress
Cataloging-in-Publication Data**

Stille, Darlene R.
Extraordinary women scientists/by Darlene Stille.
   p.   cm. — (Extraordinary people)

ISBN 0-516-00585-5
1. Women scientists — Juvenile literature.
2. Women scientists — Biography — Juvenile
literature.
[1. Scientists. 2. Women — Biography.] I. Title.
II. Series.

Q130.S75 1995   94-38938
509.2'2 — dc20 [B]   CIP
                           AC

CONTENTS

INTRODUCTION

What makes an extraordinary woman scientist? One could argue that any woman who became a scientist before the late 1900s was extraordinary. Not only did these women face the intellectual challenges of learning physics or chemistry or biology or math, but they had to do so without encouragement from society at large — and often in the face of outright disapproval from family and friends. The prevailing wisdom held that education was wasted on women. In fact, in the late 1800s and early 1900s, too much learning was thought to be damaging to women's health.

Those women who beat the odds and got an education in science found that there were few, if any, jobs open to them. Many of the courageous, pioneering women who found jobs worked for no pay at all and suffered discriminatory indignities such as being barred from laboratories, having to enter university buildings through back doors, and being deprived of toilet facilities.

Yet, hundreds of women overcame these hardships and made important contributions to the advancement of science. Although many contributed to the slow and steady accumulation of laboratory and statistical data so necessary for building a body of scientific knowledge, their contributions attracted scant attention. Few who played key roles in major discoveries that literally changed the world were rewarded with major honors.

Choosing from a long list of scientists qualified to be included in this book was no easy task. Most of the fifty women who were selected are deceased. They, as well as their contemporary counterparts, have accomplished significant "firsts" in their fields or made definitive contributions, that, in many cases, have led to Nobel Prizes. Their stories were gleaned from a wide variety of primary and secondary sources and represent a broad range of historical periods, scientific disciplines, ethnic backgrounds, and lifestyles. The women, who excelled in fields from astronomy to particle physics and from botany to neurobiology, made their contributions on nearly every continent of the world — Africa, Asia, Europe, and the Americas.

Some stayed single, others married and raised large families. Some chose an active social life, others preferred to live in solitude. They were widows, orphans, working mothers, or single parents. And some were physically challenged. In short, these extraordinary women scientists came from all walks of life. Their biographies reflect the nature and significance of their contributions to science as well as details of their personal lives and the cultural influences affecting them.

The inspiration for this book sprang from the realization that these scientists are role models for today's young women. Although the education of women in industrialized nations, in general, is no longer considered a waste, the message that girls and women are not suited for science and math is still prevalent. One of the purposes of this book is to prove that this negative message is nothing more than a myth. It seems safe to say that from the level of activity among women scientists doing research today, many exciting contributions from them are yet to come.

For ease of access, the biographies in this book appear in alphabetical order. Four additional articles provide a broad summary of the contributions of women in early science and in the fields of medicine, mathematics, and engineering — areas that will be the focus of a future collection of biographies of extraordinary women scientists.

Women Scientists from Ancient Times to the Age of Reason

Although women throughout history have been assigned an inferior status and generally denied the educational and professional opportunities granted to men, women did emerge as major contributors to scientific thought, given the right set of circumstances. Scientific thought, as people in the West understand it, originated in ancient Greece about 2,500 years ago. But long before that, human beings struggled to make sense of the world around them — and the heavens above. Their early attempts at understanding were often a mix of magic and mathematics. This was certainly true of Aglaonike of Thessaly, a sorceress who may have been the first woman astronomer. No one knows exactly when she lived, but a very old Greek legend told of her magical powers and how she could frighten and control people by "bringing down the moon from heaven." The Greek writer Plutarch, who lived around A.D. 46 to 120, interpreted this to mean that Aglaonike had a thorough knowledge of the moon and could predict when eclipses would occur.

While some early knowledge was cloaked as magic, other knowledge came from solving very practical problems. This was true of what might be regarded as early applied chemistry, in which women appear to have played important roles. For example, historians discovered that women were involved in perfume-making in Mesopotamia some 3,200 years ago. Making perfume, like tanning leather and refining metals, involves a basic chemical understanding of materials and how they react with one another. In ancient Egypt, the female deity

Isis was the goddess of many realms, including the *Kemet*, or "black earth." The word *chemistry* may have its roots in the word *Kemet*.

After western science with its rational, logical theories to explain observed phenomena arose in ancient Greece, the Greeks solved such complex problems as how to measure the circumference of Earth. They even theorized that matter was made up of tiny units called atoms. These rational thinkers did not, however, call themselves "scientists." They were known as "natural philosophers," a term that remained in use into the 1800s.

The first well-documented female natural philosopher was Hypatia, born in A.D. 370 in Alexandria, Egypt, one of the greatest cities of that time. Her father was an astronomer and mathematician and perhaps the director of the museum at Alexandria, where Hypatia received her education in the best rational Greek traditions. Hypatia's fame as a mathematician, philosopher, and teacher was known throughout the ancient world. Sadly, her life was well documented not because of her achievements, but because of her death in 415. Hypatia was brutally murdered by a mob. The murder motive is not clear but may have involved rival political or religious factions.

The scientific writings and advances made by the ancient Greeks were almost lost when Europe entered the Dark Ages — a term once used to describe the early Middle Ages. This period, from the A.D. 400s to the 900s was dominated by the Christian Church and its focus on the next life rather than this one. But progress was made in certain areas. The foundations of modern chemistry were laid during the Middle Ages by alchemists — practitioners of a mysterious art that blended religion, magic, and crude technology in a quest to transform lead and other metals into gold, and to find the elixir of life (a substance that would cure ills and lead to longer life). While most alchemists were men, historians have found evidence of a number of notable women alchemists. The earliest of these were Mary the Jewess and Cleopatra (no relation to Egypt's Queen Cleopatra), women who probably lived in the first century A.D. Mary has been credited with inventing a number of devices that proved to be important in chemistry as well as alchemy. These include the three-part still, with copper tubing for distilling liquids, and the water bath, or double boiler. Cleopatra wrote a text that was widely used as a reference among alchemists. Building on the experiments of the alchemists, the first chemists in the 1600s began to explore the nature of liquids and gases and identify the various chemical elements.

Also during the Middle Ages, the education of women was advanced in convents — Catholic institutions that provided schooling for nuns and upper-class girls. Sometimes creative scientific thinking flourished in the convents. For example, Hildegard von Bingen, a German thinker and writer in the 1100s on topics ranging from cosmology to medicine, was the abbess of a convent.

Eventually, a number of factors came together to spell the end of the Middle Ages and the beginning of the Renaissance in Europe. One of these was the rediscovery of the ancient Greek texts by European knights who set forth in the 1100s and 1200s on a series of unsuccessful crusades to win back the Holy Land from Muslim Turks. These knights discovered that the ancient Greek texts had been preserved by Islamic scholars. The knights brought the texts back to Europe, where they were translated and copied by scholars at the new universities that had been established around the great cathedrals of Europe.

Thus, rational scientific thinking was reborn in Europe, and whenever they had the opportunity, women played important roles in this rebirth. The best opportunities for women were first provided in Italy, where women could study and teach at universities even during the Middle Ages. Italian women contributed greatly to the development of anatomy. Alessandra Giliani, an anatomist at the University of Bologna in the early 1300s, reportedly found a way to trace blood vessels in cadavers by injecting the vessels with colored liquids that solidified.

Eventually, European scholars broke free of the teaching of the ancient Greeks and expanded their knowledge with experiments and more complete theories about the natural world. A great revolution began in astronomy in 1543, when Polish mathematician Nicolaus Copernicus put forth his theory that the sun, not the Earth as the Greeks believed, was the center of the solar system. His theory was supported by the observations of Danish astronomer Tycho Brahe, whose studies of the motions of planets led to far more precise tables for predicting the positions of the planets. But Brahe was assisted in his work by his sister, Sophia Brahe. And no one can be certain how much she contributed to the data that were later used by Brahe's assistant, Johannes Kepler, to discover that the planets orbit the sun in ellipses, or ovals.

Other women may have played major roles in scientific advances attributed solely to men.

One of these was Marie Anne Lavoisier, the brilliant and well-educated wife of the great French chemist Antoine Lavoisier. The couple had no children and devoted themselves to scientific studies. Antoine Lavoisier is credited with discovering that a substance in air is consumed during the process of combustion. Lavoisier called the substance "oxygen." Lavoisier and another French scientist later found that breathing and respiration in humans and other animals involves oxygen in a reaction that is similar to combustion. In 1789 Lavoisier published what some consider to be the first chemistry textbook, *The Elements of Chemistry*. Madame Lavoisier, an accomplished artist, provided the sketches and diagrams that accompanied the text.

How much Marie Anne contributed to Antoine Lavoisier's actual discoveries may never be known. But if not for her, much of Lavoisier's work may never have been presented to the world. The Lavoisiers were victims of the Reign of Terror, a violent phase toward the end of the French Revolution. A group of radicals seized control of the government in 1793 and beheaded 18,000 people. The Lavoisiers were both arrested. Marie was released, but Antoine was executed in 1794. Madame Lavoisier edited and completed the memoirs that he had begun in 1792 and saw to it that they were published.

The 1700s in Europe were called the Age of Reason or the Enlightenment. Enlightenment thinkers were greatly influenced by such discoveries as the laws of motion authored by Sir Isaac Newton in England. They believed in a mathematical thought process that set forth self-evident truths, or axioms, and logically progressed from one axiom to another. During the Age of Reason, upper-class women in England, France, and Italy took an active interest in science.

Individuals such as the English Duchess Margaret Cavendish (1623-1673) helped make science a fashionable topic for study among ladies.

The methods of reason also gave rise to the first logical argument in favor of equality for women. A British writer named Mary Wollstonecraft argued in her book, *A Vindication of the Rights of Woman* (1792), that women are intellectually equal to men and could be happier and make greater contributions to society if they had better educational opportunities.

As an example of how far an educated woman could go, Caroline Herschel, sister of the German astronomer William Herschel, in the late 1700s discovered nebulae and comets and completed a star catalog for the British Royal Society. Her family had denied her an education, but her brother gave her lessons in mathematics and astronomy.

The idea of educating women took hold in the 1800s but focused on skills that would make women charming companions and good mothers. Although women were encouraged to attend finishing schools, universities were closed to them in the United States and Europe — even in Italy. Not only was education for women considered a waste of time and money, because women were "intellectually inferior beings," but the idea took hold that too much learning would damage a woman's health.

The opening up of educational and career opportunities in the sciences and other areas did not begin in earnest until the rise of the first women's rights movement in the mid-1800s and the radical struggle in the early 1900s to earn women the right to vote. On the wave of this feminist movement, women in the late 1800s and early 1900s began to break through as scientific pioneers.

MARY ANNING

1799-1847
Fossil Hunter

Mary Anning had no formal training as a scientist. Nevertheless, her keen eyesight and excellent powers of observation made her one of the most successful fossil hunters of the early 1800s. She was so good, in fact, that a local legend attributed her achievements to supernatural powers. According to the tale, Mary Anning's nurse was taking her out in a baby carriage one day when a bolt of lightning struck. The nurse was killed, and Mary was left with the supernatural gift of finding rare fossils of long-extinct creatures embedded in the rocky cliffs that line the English coast.

Mary Anning was born in 1799 in the English resort town of Lyme Regis, where beautiful coiled fossil shells washed out of the cliffs onto the beach. Local people merely gathered up the "curiosities" and sold them to visiting tourists. At first, no one knew what these objects were. Later, however, through the efforts of Mary Anning, scientists discovered that the fossil "curiosities" represented the first evidence of the Age of Dinosaurs. The shells, which are now called ammonites, were the fossil remains of prehistoric mollusks that thrived in the warm seas of the Jurassic Period, which began 205 million years ago. As the mollusks died, they were buried in the sediments on the seafloor. Millions of years later, these sediments hardened into rock, the sea level fell, and the rocky cliffs were exposed. Eventually, erosion by wind and water revealed the fossils entombed in the rock layers, and they gradually washed down to the beach.

Mary Anning's interest in shells began when her father — a cabinetmaker by trade — started collecting shells as a hobby. Often, Mary and her brother accompanied him to the beach, where Mary soon became a skilled curiosity hunter herself. One morning in 1811, after a terrible storm, Mary went to the beach expecting to find a new supply of fossils washed away from the rocky cliffs. What she found was more than a few coiled shells. To her surprise, a fossilized skeleton lay on the beach. It looked like a huge sea dragon, but it was actually a prehistoric sea reptile resembling a modern porpoise. Word about her remarkable discovery spread quickly. Scientists and professors came to look at the creature, and eventually a museum bought it from Anning. It was named *Ichthyosaurus*, meaning "fish lizard."

With the income Anning was getting from selling fossils and a small grant from the government, she devoted herself full-time to fossil research. Her reputation as a serious fossil hunter spread with news of another wonderful find — a sea monster with four long, pointed flippers, a short tail, and a long neck. This one was named *Plesiosaurus*, meaning "near lizard," because it resembled a lizard more than a fish.

In 1828, Anning discovered the fossil of yet another prehistoric monster. But this creature

did not live in the sea. It had wings and was believed to be a flying dragon that had once glided through the skies of the Jurassic Period. The fossil bones were studied by an Oxford University professor who named it *Pterodactyl*, meaning "wing finger."

Anning's skill in finding fossils attracted many visitors to Lyme Regis. When she died of cancer in 1847, her death proved to be an economic loss to the town as the number of visitors dropped off. But the fossil treasures she preserved for future generations of scientists to study are wealth beyond measure.

FLORENCE AUGUSTA MERRIAM BAILEY

1863-1948
Ornithologist

 They traveled as far as they could go by train. Then they boarded covered wagons and headed off on rutted trails into the newly opened American West. Often, Florence Bailey and her husband Vernon rode on horseback with a pack train into mountainous regions, setting up primitive campsites. Nothing stopped them in their travels. They were determined to explore the desolate areas of Arizona, New Mexico, Texas, and the Dakotas to research indigenous wildlife. And their determination paid off. In time, Florence Bailey became a famous ornithologist, known not only for her ability to make observations about the birds of an area but also to describe them in beautifully written detail. She was a tireless promoter of the Audubon Society, an organization dedicated to the protection and wise use of wildlife, land, water, and natural resources.

Florence Merriam was born on August 8, 1863, in the rural village of Locust Grove, New York, near the western foothills of the Adirondacks. She was the youngest of four children. Her father was a merchant and banker, then a U.S. congressman. Her mother had been educated at Rutgers Female Institute in New York City. Florence grew up and received her early education on the family's country estate — Homewood. There she learned to observe and love nature and wildlife. After attending Mrs. Pratt's Seminary, a preparatory school in Utica, New York, she enrolled at Smith College for Women. She studied English from 1882 to 1886 but left the school without taking a degree.

Like many educated young women in the 1890s, Florence Merriam was interested in social work and the issues it addressed. Committed to helping European immigrants who were living in urban slums surrounded by disease, poverty, and crime, Merriam went first to Chicago, Illinois, and then to New York City. In Chicago she spent a summer month at a school for working girls near Jane Addams's Hull House. Next she helped out at a working girls' club in New York City. Unfortunately, while engaged in these activities, she was infected with tuberculosis (TB), a serious lung disease.

Doctors now know that tuberculosis is caused by a bacterium and can be treated with antibiotics. But in the 1890s, the only treatment was plenty of clean, fresh air, so Florence Merriam went to live in the southwestern United States. While resting, she kept busy observing bird life and writing about the natural world of the Southwest, which was very different from the natural world she had observed in the Northeast. In 1896, the year she was pronounced cured of TB, she published her first book, *A-birding on a Bronco*. Florence then went to live in Washington, D.C., with her brother, the first chief of the U.S. Biological Survey. There she met Vernon Bailey, a biologist for the Survey, whom she married in December 1899.

Because the Baileys were childless, Florence accompanied Vernon when the government sent him on field trips to record the mammals, reptiles, and plants of the West. She used the opportunity to record her observations of bird life. One of her best-known works, *Handbook*

of Birds of the Western United States, was published in 1902. In 1928, she completed a work on the southwestern birds called *Birds of New Mexico*. In 1931 it won for her the Brewster Medal of the American Ornithologists' Union. For two of her husband's books, *Wild Animals of Glacier National Park* (1918) and *Cave Life of Kentucky* (1933), she wrote the sections on birds. Her last major work was *Among the Birds in the Grand Canyon National Park* (1939).

When the Baileys were at their home in Washington, D.C., they hosted gatherings of both professional and amateur naturalists. Florence helped found the Audubon Society of the District of Columbia and conducted classes there for schoolteachers. Vernon Bailey died in 1942, and Florence six years later on September 22, 1948.

FLORENCE BASCOM

1862-1945
Geologist

It may have seemed peculiar for the daughter of a university president to ride horseback into the hills and mountains of Pennsylvania, Maryland, and New Jersey just to dig among rocks. But that is what it took for Florence Bascom to analyze the formations of the Mid-Atlantic Piedmont — her assignment as the first woman geologist employed by the U.S. Geological Survey. Her work helped geologists understand how the Appalachians and their foothills formed. She was not only a pioneer in the field of geology, but she was also an inspiring teacher who established a geology department at Bryn Mawr College and encouraged future generations of women to enter a profession that had until then been dominated by men.

Florence Bascom was born on July 14, 1862, in Williamstown, Massachusetts, the youngest of three children of John and Emma Bascom. Her mother was a schoolteacher, artist, and activist in the suffrage movement that won voting rights for women. Her father, a school administrator, became president of the University of Wisconsin at Madison in 1874. With parents such as these, Florence was surely encouraged to pursue higher education.

She enrolled at the University of Wisconsin in 1877, at a time when higher education for women was still a rather new idea. The school had been admitting women students only since 1872, and it had some peculiar notions about coeducation. For example, men and women had to use the library on alternate days, and if a classroom was full, men were given preference over women.

In spite of these obvious inequalities, and because of Florence Bascom's ability and determination, she received three bachelor's degrees from the university — one in the arts and one in letters in 1882, then one in science in 1884. Her interest in geology, particularly petrology, which is the study of rock composition and how the major types of rock form, led her to acquire a master's degree in geology in 1887. After receiving her master's, Bascom taught for two years at Rockford College in Illinois, and then returned to school for her doctoral degree. One of the first women students at Johns Hopkins University in Baltimore, Maryland, she became the first woman to earn a Ph.D. in petrology in 1893. After teaching at Ohio State University for two years, she began her association with two institutions that, eventually, defined her career — Bryn Mawr College and the U.S. Geological Survey (USGS).

In 1896, Bascom was hired by the USGS as an assistant geologist, the first woman to hold such a post. The USGS was in the process of creating geological maps of various areas in the United States. The information collected was intended to help locate oil and valuable minerals and to shed light on the geological processes that created mountains and other formations.

Bascom was assigned to the Piedmont Region bordering the Appalachian Mountains. She did fieldwork during the summer, riding into remote areas with horse and buggy or on horseback, studying the rock formations and collecting rock samples. During the winter, she spent long hours analyzing the mineral composition of the rocks with a special microscope. Her reports, which contained highly technical information about the rocks and the processes that formed them, were published in USGS bulletins.

While providing this important fieldwork, Bascom was also busy trying to establish a geology department at Bryn Mawr College. She developed a rock collection and a geological library from scratch. Because geology was not considered a useful course of study for young women at this time, she had to convince the college administration to make geology part of the curriculum. Only after threatening to resign did Bascom succeed in establishing geology as a major.

In 1906, she became a full professor in geology at Bryn Mawr. Under her guidance, several distinguished women geologists received their training there. Her students included Ida Ogilvie, who built up a geology department at Barnard College; Julia Gardner, a paleontologist who studied fossils and sediments in oil-rich rocks on the Gulf Coast; and Eleanora Bliss Knopf and Anna Jonas Stose, who worked on analyzing a type of break in rock called a thrust fault, which later became important in the study of earthquakes and mountain ranges.

During her lifetime, Florence Bascom received professional recognition for her achievements. She was a member of many scientific associations and became the first woman elected to the Geological Society of America, serving as its vice president in 1930. She became professor emeritus in 1928 and retired from the USGS in 1936, remaining actively involved in geology until her death on June 18, 1945.

Jocelyn Bell Burnell

1943-
Astronomer

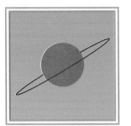

It was not your ordinary telescope. It consisted of a thousand poles about nine feet tall from which Jocelyn Bell and her student colleagues strung miles of wires and cables over a 4½-acre area near Cambridge University in England. This telescope was designed to listen for radio signals from deepest space. Jocelyn Bell then analyzed the data coming in and being recorded by automatic pens on rolls of paper. In the course of this work, she made an astounding discovery: There are stars so small and dense that they complete a spin in little more than a second and give off beams of intense radio waves. These stars were named pulsars. Their discovery rocked the scientific world and earned Bell's advising professor at Cambridge University a Nobel Prize.

Susan Jocelyn Bell was born on July 15, 1943, in Belfast, Northern Ireland, and raised in the countryside. She was the oldest of four children born to M. Allison and G. Philip Bell, an architect. The Bell family, originally from Scotland, came to Ireland in the 1700s. Ireland had long been plagued by conflicts between Catholics and Protestants, but the Bells were Quakers, a pacifist denomination that shuns war and armed conflict. They also embrace the idea of equal rights for all, including women.

Until she was thirteen years old, Jocelyn attended the local school. But when she took an examination to determine whether she would go to college or to a trade school, Jocelyn flunked. She attributed her failure to the fact that she was quite young, a slow developer, and had not received an adequate education in the local schools. Realizing Jocelyn's potential, her parents sent her to a Quaker boarding school in England where she got a second chance.

Through her father, Jocelyn got to know the staff at the Armagh Observatory in Northern Ireland and became interested in astronomy. In 1961, she entered the University of Glasgow in Scotland, where she majored in physics and graduated with honors in 1965. She then went on to work for a Ph.D. in astronomy at Cambridge University.

Her supervising professor at Cambridge, Anthony Hewish, was a radioastronomer. By the 1960s, astronomers were building telescopes that could "see" in areas of the electromagnetic spectrum other than visible light. The electromagnetic spectrum is the range of radiation from high-energy gamma rays and X rays through infrared, visible, and ultraviolet light to microwaves and low-energy radio waves. Hewish planned to build a radiotelescope that would detect a particular wavelength of radio waves given off by objects in deep space. Bell, one of Hewish's graduate students, was given the task of helping to build the telescope and then overseeing its operation and analyzing the data it collected.

Instead of capturing images from light waves on photographic plates or film, the radio-telescope translated the radio waves it detected into lines made by pens moving across rolls of paper. Bell pored over thousands of feet of paper, trying to differentiate between radio waves generated by stars in space and radio waves generated by people on Earth. One day in October 1967, she noticed an unusual pattern of lines. Looking further, she found that this pattern reappeared in keeping with sidereal time, the time set by the stars. (Earth rotates every 24 hours in relation to the sun, but only every 23 hours and 56 minutes in relation to the stars.) This small but crucial difference told Bell that this particular signal was coming from deep space. In addition to an unusual pattern of lines, Bell also noted that the radio waves were pulsing, or sending out bursts of energy, every $1\frac{1}{3}$ seconds.

Bell alerted Hewish. At first he did not believe that these bursts of radio waves were coming from space. He thought they must be coming from some radio transmitter on Earth. But convincing measurements made by radio astronomers indicated that the pulses were coming from a source 200 light-years away. (The vast distances of space are measured in light-years — the distance light travels in one year, or 5.9 trillion miles.) The astronomers also believed that the pulses were coming from a small body, perhaps a planet of another star. This led them to wonder briefly whether the signals were coming from an intelligent life form. But when Bell found a similar set of bursts coming from another region of the sky, she said it was unlikely that "little green men" on two distant planets were trying to contact Earth. Later, she found two more of these odd objects, which the press dubbed "pulsars."

Today, astronomers believe that pulsars are rapidly rotating objects called neutron stars, which form when a huge star runs out of nuclear fuel. Without the heat and pressure from nuclear reactions to resist the force of gravity, all the matter in the star collapses inward. Then

a gigantic explosion, called a supernova, blasts away the outer layers of the star. What remains is a core of subatomic particles so dense that the equivalent of all the matter contained in our sun is packed into a ball about 6 miles in diameter.

A neutron star spins so fast and has such a strong magnetic field that it sets up an electric field powerful enough to rip subatomic particles from the surface of the star. In doing so, a beam of radio waves is created. Like a lighthouse beacon, this beam sweeps across space and is detectable from Earth with every rotation of the neutron star — once or twice a second.

After discovering pulsars, Bell earned her Ph.D., married in 1968, and then left the field of radioastronomy. She followed her husband, a government official, when he moved from one post to another. She worked part-time in teaching and in astronomy while raising their son, who was diagnosed with juvenile diabetes at the age of ten. The pain of learning to cope with chronic illness led her to write a thought-provoking book, *Broken for Life* (1989). Soon afterward, she and her husband divorced.

For her discovery of pulsars, Bell Burnell received critical acclaim. In 1973, she and Hewish were awarded the prestigious Albert A. Michelson Medal of the Franklin Institute of Philadelphia. Bell Burnell also won awards from the American Astronomical Society and the Royal Astronomical Society. When Hewish, not Bell Burnell, won a Nobel Prize in 1974, many astronomers thought she was at least as deserving as he. But Bell Burnell said, "Nobel Prizes are based on long-standing research, not a flash-in-the-pan observation of a research student. Giving the award to me would have debased the prize."

In 1991, Bell Burnell moved to Milton Keynes to take a full-time job as professor of physics in Britain's Open University, an institution that admits adults regardless of their high school grades or previous background. To her students, the Open University represents a second chance at obtaining a higher education. To Jocelyn Bell Burnell, it represents a return to a full-time career in science.

RUTH FULTON BENEDICT
1887-1948
Anthropologist

Ruth Benedict had an extremely difficult childhood, beset by poverty and emotional strain. To make matters worse, a measles infection, which she contracted as an infant, severely damaged her hearing. For years, she suffered from serious bouts of depression. But she was a brilliant young woman. She rose above her physical and emotional handicaps to become the leading American anthropologist in the 1930s and a mentor for such other leaders in the field as Margaret Mead.

Ruth Fulton was born in New York City on June 5, 1887, into a family with a very promising future. Her father, Frederick, was a surgeon and cancer researcher. Her mother, Bertrice, was a graduate of Vassar College. But before Ruth was two years old, circumstances changed radically for the family. Her father died suddenly, leaving her mother to raise Ruth and her three-month-old sister alone. Forced to take teaching jobs wherever she could, Ruth's mother moved the girls first to Norwich, New York, where their grandparents had a farm; then to St. Joseph, Missouri; and then to Owatonna, Minnesota. In 1899, she accepted a job as a librarian in Buffalo, New York, where the family finally settled down.

Her mother's excessive grief after the loss of her husband had a very negative effect on Ruth, who took refuge in an imaginary world and comfort from an imaginary playmate. Yet, Ruth did very well in school, winning scholarships to a preparatory school and then to Vassar College, where she studied English literature.

After graduating in 1909, Ruth went to Europe with friends. Upon returning to the United States, she worked for a charitable organization in Buffalo, New York, and then taught school in California. In 1914 she quit work to marry a biochemist named Stanley R. Benedict. Unable to have children, Ruth felt useless sitting idly around the house. She began questioning the traditional role of women as nonworking housewives. While writing biographies of women, she began formulating ideas about the differences between male and female personalities. Her strong feminist ideas clashed with those of her husband, eventually leading her to seek a job outside the home. The arguments that followed strained their relationship, and although they continued to live together for a number of years, their marriage was never the same. For a time, Ruth wrote poetry under the pen name Anne Singleton. Then in 1919 she enrolled in the New School for Social Research in New York City. This event signaled the beginning of a new life for her.

Fascinated with the science of anthropology, which was still in its early stages of development, Ruth Benedict continued her studies at Columbia University under the famed anthropologist Franz Boas. After receiving a Ph.D. in 1923, she did fieldwork among several Native American tribes, including the Zuni and Blackfoot. She focused on how cultural themes, such as the idea of a guardian spirit, varied from tribe to tribe. Even at this time she was interested in how cultures shape individual experiences and personalities.

In the 1920s, new psychoanalytical theories about individual personalities were being promoted. Benedict expanded on these theories by suggesting that cultures have unique personalities, too. The idea that cultures could be described in the terms people used to describe individual personalities was new and grabbed the public imagination, even if scientists later questioned it.

Using certain Native American cultures of the Southwest as examples, Benedict claimed that while one culture was reserved and dignified, another was more flamboyant. She called her theory "personality writ large" and explained it in her 1934 book, *Patterns of Culture*, which described and contrasted the very different personalities of different cultures and at the same time drew lessons from them about society. Eventually, *Patterns of Culture* was translated into fourteen languages. For many years it was the most popular introductory text to anthropology.

During World War II (1939-1945), Benedict took up the study of race as well as culture. In 1940, she wrote against racism in the context of Nazi Germany. Her book, called *Race: Science and Politics*, proposed that societies could use the insights of anthropology to foster positive change. In 1941, when the United States entered World War II, she worked at the Office of War Information (Bureau of Overseas Intelligence) writing anthropological reports on allied and enemy nations. Her final cross-cultural study involved analyzing Japan. In 1946, after Japan's defeat, Benedict wrote a famous anthropological analysis, *The Chrysanthemum and the Sword: Patterns of Japanese Culture*, which she hoped would aid in planning "a wise postwar policy" and help bring about lasting change.

For most of her professional career, Benedict was associated with Columbia University. But because she was a woman, it was not until late in life that she received academic recognition. From 1922 to 1931, she lectured in anthropology and served as Franz Boas's assistant. One of her first students was Margaret Mead, who in 1959 chronicled Benedict's life and work in *An Anthropologist at Work: Writings of Ruth Benedict*. What began as a teacher-student relationship between Benedict and Mead, soon developed into friendship and then mutual support as colleagues. The relationship had a positive effect on their individual contributions to anthropology. The communication between them helped Benedict clarify her anthropological views and approaches and focus on her "female nature."

Because Franz Boas did not believe married women needed much money, he did not help Benedict gain a permanent appointment as an assistant professor at Columbia until she separated from her husband in 1930. From 1925 to 1940, Benedict served as editor of the *Journal of American Folklore*. In 1936, after Boas retired, she was promoted to associate professor and for the next three years served as acting director of the department of anthropology. After working on national character studies in Washington, D.C., from 1943 to 1946, Benedict returned to Columbia University to direct the Research in Contemporary Cultures project funded by the U.S. Navy. Later, she was also elected president of the American Anthropological Association.

Columbia University made Ruth Fulton Benedict a full professor in 1948, but, unfortunately, she had little time to enjoy the distinction. On September 17, 1948, after returning from a visit to Europe, Ruth Benedict suffered a heart attack and died. After her death, professional anthropologists criticized her work and often disregarded it as weak and ineffectual. They claimed that her characterizations of cultures were based too much on impressions and not enough on facts. More recently, however, anthropologists have been acknowledging the strengths of Benedict's particular anthropological approach and the significance of her theory that both personal and political conditions shape society.

ANNIE JUMP CANNON

1863-1941
Astronomer

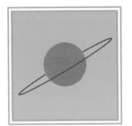

It was young Annie Jump Cannon's mother who first introduced her to the stars. From the attic of their home in Dover, Delaware, Annie and her mother enjoyed gazing at the night sky. Using an old astronomy textbook, they tried to identify the stars. Annie memorized the constellations, observed how the positions of the stars changed from season to season, and recorded her notes by candlelight. Thus, her fascination with the heavens began, a passion that eventually led her to the Harvard College Observatory, where she created one of the greatest catalogs of stars ever produced. Annie did this work in a world of silence, because by the time she became a Harvard astronomer, she was almost completely deaf.

When Annie Jump Cannon was born in Dover, Delaware, on December 11, 1863, the United States was embroiled in Civil War. Just a month before, President Abraham Lincoln had delivered his famous Gettysburg Address. Annie's father, Wilson Lee Cannon, had played a role in the beginning of the Civil War, when as a member of Delaware's Senate he cast the deciding vote that kept Delaware in the Union.

Annie grew up in a large household with six other children, including four stepbrothers and stepsisters. Her mother, Mary Elizabeth, was her father's second wife. Because Annie's father was a wealthy shipbuilder and politician, she never had to worry about money for her education. And when her teachers recommended that she go to college, her parents without hesitation agreed.

In 1880, Annie Jump Cannon enrolled at Wellesley College in Massachusetts, one of several U.S. colleges for women. Highly interested in astronomy, Cannon became influenced by Sarah F. Whiting, one of the first important women professors of physics and astronomy. Whiting introduced Cannon to spectroscopy — a technique that analyzes light coming from the stars — and taught her how to use a spectroscope — an instrument containing a prism that separates light into its various colors. By this time, astronomers had concluded that spectroscopy provided a wonderful tool for learning about the distant stars, because each chemical element heated by the energy in a star emits, or gives off, its own unique pattern of light.

It is believed that Cannon contracted an illness that damaged her hearing during her first year at Wellesley. Reportedly, she had one upper respiratory infection after another. And because she was accustomed to the mild winters in Delaware, she was not prepared for the harsh Massachusetts weather. She brought only thin-soled shoes and a light overcoat, garments that provided little warmth or comfort for a young woman with a fever, cough, and earache. For whatever reason, after her first year at Wellesley, Cannon suffered a progressive hearing loss.

After graduating in 1884, Cannon returned to her family home and to the elegant activities of Dover society. Although vivacious and popular, she showed no interest in settling down to married life. Instead, she embarked for Europe with her "Kamerette," one of the first box cameras. Her experience with photography would later prove invaluable to her work in astronomy.

In 1893, Cannon returned to Wellesley to work on a master's degree and then enrolled as a special student of astronomy at Radcliffe College. In 1896, she joined astronomy professors Edward C. Pickering and Williamina Fleming on the staff of the Harvard College Observatory.

Pickering, who was director, and Fleming had been engaged in a massive project to photograph and analyze the spectra of stars. Using their system for classifying stars according to their spectra, Cannon developed what became known as the Harvard System of Spectral Classification. Her system used letters and Roman numerals to rank stars from the hottest white and blue stars to the coolest red stars. She found that almost all the stars in the visible sky, from the North Pole to the South Pole, fit these groupings.

In 1911, Cannon succeeded Williamina Fleming as Harvard's curator of astronomical photographs. She held the post until 1938, when she was appointed the William Cranch Bond Astronomer at Harvard University. During her long career, she received many honors, including an honorary Doctor of Science degree from Oxford University in England, the first awarded to a woman. She received the National Academy of Science Draper Medal but was never elected to the National Academy. After winning the Ellen Richards Research Prize in 1932, Cannon established the Annie Jump Cannon Prize of the American Astronomical Society, presented every three years to an outstanding woman astronomer.

Annie Jump Cannon indulged her fondness for entertaining in her home, Star Cottage, near the observatory. She was noted for her children's parties, especially her annual Easter eggrolling contest. She was also politically active in the suffrage movement, which eventually gained women the right to vote.

Annie Jump Cannon retired from Harvard in 1940 and died of heart failure on April 13, 1941. Perhaps her greatest achievement was the creation of a huge, nine-volume work called *The Henry Draper Catalogue*, named after a pioneer in stellar spectroscopy. In this catalog and several smaller works, Cannon classified about 350,000 stars. Skillful at examining complex photographic plates, she could classify more than three stars a minute. She also discovered about 300 variable stars — stars whose light varies in brightness. Her works have served as invaluable references for other astronomers.

EMMA PERRY CARR

1880-1972
Physical Chemist

The words *teamwork* and *empowerment* were not part of everyday vocabulary in 1913. But those were the principles that Emma Perry Carr applied to her new research program in the chemistry department at Mount Holyoke College, a school for women in South Hadley, Massachusetts. As head of the department, Carr believed that both the school and its students would benefit if faculty and students worked together to solve difficult scientific problems. The problems she selected involved analyzing carbon compounds with ultraviolet light, one of the most difficult research tasks of that scientific era. As a result of this team process, Carr's impressive accomplishments in chemical research won recognition and honors not only for herself but also for the entire Mount Holyoke chemistry department.

Emma Perry Carr was born on July 23, 1880, in Holmesville, Ohio. She and her two brothers and two sisters had many opportunities. The Carrs were a fairly prosperous family; both her father and her grandfather were physicians. When it came time for Emma to go to college, she first attended Ohio State University, then Mount Holyoke, and finally the University of Chicago, where she received her bachelor of science degree in chemistry in 1905. She taught at Mount Holyoke from 1905 to 1908, then returned to the University of Chicago to earn a Ph.D. in chemistry in 1910. She then joined the faculty of Mount Holyoke College, where she remained throughout her career, becoming a full professor and head of the chemistry department in 1913.

Carr was fascinated with physical chemistry, the branch of chemistry concerned with the structure and behavior of atoms and molecules. At that time, scientists were just beginning to understand in detail how atoms bond together to form molecules. Based on the new theories of atomic structure, chemists believed that the electrons orbiting each atomic nucleus were responsible for chemical bonds between the atoms. Some of the most complex bonds were those found in organic compounds, molecules containing carbon atoms. To explore the nature of these bonds, Carr turned to a technique called absorption spectroscopy. The process involved exposing a chemical sample to electromagnetic radiation, such as ultraviolet light, and detecting the wavelengths of light that the sample absorbed. This information provided insights into the strengths and locations of chemical bonds because electrons absorb light.

Carr was one of the first scientists in the United States to become an expert in this highly technical field of research. She traveled to Northern Ireland in 1919 and to Switzerland in the 1920s to work with scientists who had mastered spectroscopic techniques. Then she

returned to Mount Holyoke, where she instituted a new approach to research. Firmly believing that participating in research was an essential part of teaching and learning, she involved teams of students and faculty members in an effort to solve the problem of synthesizing and analyzing organic molecules with ultraviolet light. Ultimately, her research teams made important contributions to the understanding of molecular structure in hydrocarbons and to the nature of the carbon-carbon bond.

Many of Carr's students went on to become renowned professors and researchers. One of her former students wrote that "Throughout the country and in practically every women's college and in many great universities [Carr's students] are to be found carrying the torch she lit for them at Mount Holyoke." Carr created such an interest in chemistry among women students that more than ninety Mount Holyoke graduates earned Ph.D's in chemistry from other institutions between 1920 and 1980.

During her career, Emma Perry Carr received several honorary doctorates and many other awards. Her research program was funded in the 1930s by grants from the National Research Council and the Rockefeller Foundation. In 1937, she became the first person to receive the Garvan Award of the American Chemical Society. After her retirement from Mount Holyoke in 1946, she was active in local politics and community affairs. At the age of eighty-four, she moved to a retirement home in Evanston, Illinois, where she remained until her death on January 7, 1972.

RACHEL LOUISE CARSON

1907-1964
Marine Biologist, Science Writer

When Rachel Carson went to college, she was faced with a hard decision. This quiet young woman had long thought that she would become a writer, so she enrolled as an English major at the Pennsylvania College for Women. But then, after taking a required course in biology, she fell in love with science. She assumed that she would have to choose one or the other — zoology or a writing career. But the life of Rachel Carson blended both — and in a way that was to alter forever how Americans and their government viewed the natural environment and society's responsibility to protect it. Rachel Carson's book, *Silent Spring*, was largely responsible for the birth of the modern environmental movement.

Rachel Carson was born on May 27, 1907, in Springdale, Pennsylvania, the youngest of two daughters and a son born to Robert and Maria Carson. Rachel's father was an insurance salesman who invested in local real estate. Her mother was a former schoolteacher. Because Rachel's brother and sister were already in school when she was born, her mother was able to devote a great deal of time to showing Rachel the beauty of nature on the family's sixty-five-acres of land. She also instilled in Rachel a deep love of books.

Rachel showed her literary talent at an early age. Her first published story appeared in a magazine when she was ten years old. In college, she felt she did not have the imagination to write fiction. After she switched her course of study from literature to science, Carson confided to a friend that biology would give her something to write about. That proved to be an incredible understatement.

Carson graduated from college in 1929 and won a scholarship to Johns Hopkins University in Baltimore, Maryland, where she earned a master's degree in zoology in 1932. She then joined the zoology department at the University of Maryland. The most significant influence on her professional career at this time, however, was her study of the ocean and its life forms at the Woods Hole Oceanographic Institution on Cape Cod, Massachusetts.

Carson's life changed radically in the mid-1930s. Her father died suddenly in 1935, leaving her mother without financial support. The next year, her sister died, leaving two young daughters, whom Carson and her mother decided to raise. With three people to support, Carson needed a better-paying job. She applied for a post as a junior aquatic biologist with the U.S. Bureau of Fisheries and became one of the first two women hired by the bureau for a nonclerical job.

In this unlikely setting, Carson's writing career took off. She wrote a series of radio programs about oceans and then wrote and edited a number of publications for the bureau. A few years after the bureau merged with another agency in 1940, becoming the U.S. Fish and Wildlife Service, Carson became chief editor of all their publications. While in the employ of the U.S. government, Carson was also writing on the side. In 1937, the *Atlantic Monthly* published her article "Undersea," a beautifully written essay about marine life. An editor at a publishing house then encouraged Carson to write a book about the sea for the general public. This she did, and *Under the Sea Wind* was published in 1941.

In 1948, Carson began work on what would become her first best-seller, *The Sea Around Us*. For this book, she gathered data from more than one thousand sources, especially ocean studies conducted during World War II. Publication of this book in 1951 made Carson famous. *The Sea Around Us* climbed to the top of the best-seller lists, where it stayed for more than a year. The book won the National Book Award, and Carson won a Guggenheim Fellowship.

With money from the book and the fellowship, Carson was able to resign from the Fish and Wildlife Service and devote herself to writing. She bought a summer home on the coast of Maine, where she could study the ecology of tide pools. Her next book, *The Edge of the Sea*, was published in 1955. It focused on the delicate web of life, pointing out the interdependence of all living creatures in seashore communities. In 1957, one of Carson's nieces died, leaving a five-year-old son whom Carson decided to raise. A year later, Carson's mother died. In the midst of this family turmoil, Carson had little time to write, until a friend with a private bird sanctuary came to Carson for help.

Carson's friend explained that a plane had flown over the bird sanctuary and sprayed DDT, a powerful pesticide. DDT-spraying was part of Massachusetts' mosquito-control program. Many birds and harmless insects were killed as a result. At the time, DDT and other pesticides were very much on the minds of Carson and other scientists. After World War II, these poisonous chemicals had come into widespread use to control insect pests. They were being sprayed everywhere, from agricultural fields to family neighborhoods. DDT and other pesticides were very popular with the public and the government because they were so effective. As a result, pesticides had become a multimillion-dollar business.

Like many other scientists of the time, Rachel Carson was concerned about what these powerful poisons were doing to the environment. She tried in vain to get various magazines interested in publishing an article on the subject. None would touch such a controversial topic. No one wanted to hear that the activities of industrial societies could cause widespread ecological damage.

Realizing how important is was to bring the issue to the public's attention, Carson decided to write a book about it. For her research, she collected facts from a broad range of experts worldwide and accumulated studies on DDT that showed effects ranging from declining bird populations to suspected increases in human cancers. Her book, *Silent Spring*, questioned the right of an industrial society to pollute at will, without regard to the effects on the environment. Carson argued that unchecked pollution would result in ever-diminishing populations of birds and other wildlife, ending someday in a "silent spring," devoid of the glorious sounds of nature reawakening

Silent Spring, published in 1962, set off a storm of controversy. The chemical industry and even some agencies of the U. S. government set out to discredit the book and its author. Their attempts to portray Carson as a crank were unsuccessful. Her message — that the indiscriminate use of pesticides and other pollutants posed a grave danger to the environment — came through loud and clear. Within a few years, the U.S. government banned the use of DDT, and the newly born environmental movement gained steadily in strength and influence.

Rachel Carson did not live to see the results of all her efforts to protect the environment. During the writing of *Silent Spring*, she had been diagnosed with breast cancer. Within two years, the cancer had spread throughout her body. On April 14, 1964, two years after publication of *Silent Spring*, Rachel Carson died.

JEWEL PLUMMER COBB

1924-
Cell Biologist, Educator

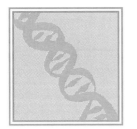

Jewel Plummer Cobb grew up in Chicago in the 1920s and 1930s, surrounded by highly successful black Americans. Racial discrimination was common in American life then, and the civil rights movement of the 1960s was more than thirty years in the future. Jewel's parents and their friends were intensely aware of the problems facing black people in a predominantly white world. Perhaps that is why they valued education highly and regarded it as an important factor in improving the lives of African Americans. The Plummers proudly followed the accomplishments of other black Americans and set high standards for their daughter. She did not disappoint them. After earning a Ph.D. in cell biology from New York University, she made important contributions to understanding skin cancer. Then, as an educator and college administrator, she worked to improve educational opportunities for women and minorities.

Jewel Plummer was born in Chicago, Illinois, on January 17, 1924, the only child of Frank Plummer, a physician, and Carriebel Cole Plummer, a dance instructor. The friends and neighbors of the Plummers were talented, successful black people — social scientists, musicians, historians, and writers. The family's social life revolved around their professional friends, their church, and their summers at Idlewild, a resort area in northern Michigan popular with African Americans.

From the time Jewel looked through a microscope as a high-school sophomore, she knew she wanted to become a biologist. After reading *The Microbe Hunters*, a book written by Paul DeKruif in 1926, there was no doubt in her mind that she would attend college. Because many of her friends from Idlewild were going to the University of Michigan in Ann Arbor, she decided to go there also.

When Jewel arrived at the university, she found a great deal of racial discrimination. Dormitories were segregated, with all black students living in one large building. Obviously, this was not a world in which she would feel comfortable. After three semesters, she transferred to Talladega College in Alabama, a black college, from which she graduated in 1944. She went on to graduate school at New York University, earning her Ph.D. in cell biology in 1950. Then she began doing research with grants from the National Cancer Institute, which continued to fund her work for more than twenty years. In 1954, Jewel married Roy Raul Cobb. They had one son, Roy Jonathon, who eventually became a physician specializing in radiology. The Cobbs divorced in 1967.

As a researcher, Jewel Plummer Cobb was interested in how individual cells behave, particularly cancer cells. She made her specialty the study of melanoma, a type of skin cancer involving melanin, the pigment that gives skin its color. (The more melanin a person has, the darker their skin will be.) Cobb learned how to grow human and mouse tumor cells in laboratory culture and then studied the effects of newly developed chemotherapeutic agents on the cells. Because cancer is the wild and uncontrolled growth of cells, she investigated factors that control cell growth and also the role that genes play.

Cobb continued her research while teaching at various schools. From 1952 to 1954, she taught at the University of Illinois medical school, then at the New York University medical school, where she stayed until 1960. From 1960 to 1969, she was a professor of biology at Sarah Lawrence College. Afterward, she began to move into administrative positions. In 1969, she became a dean and professor of zoology at Connecticut College and in 1976, dean and professor of biological sciences at Douglass College of Rutgers University.

In 1981, Cobb was appointed president of California State University at Fullerton, a post she held until 1990, when she became emeritus president, professor of biology, and trustee professor. In all her various administrative posts, she encouraged women and minorities to go into science and medicine and developed special programs for this purpose.

Jewel Plummer Cobb has served on the boards of numerous community, government, and business organizations and received many awards for her accomplishments, including twenty honorary degrees. The Bunting-Cobb Mathematics and Science Hall for Women at Douglass College was named in her honor as were the Jewel Plummer Cobb Residence Halls at California State University, in Fullerton.

GERTY RADNITZ CORI

1896-1957
Biochemist

When Gerty Radnitz was sixteen years old, she decided that she wanted to go to medical school. In the early 1900s, the university medical school in Prague was open to women, but it presented a problem for Gerty. Her previous education — private tutors and a girls' finishing school — did not prepare her for the tough entrance exams that she would have to pass. She learned that she needed the equivalent of eight years of Latin, five years of math, and a good background in chemistry and physics. Rather than being discouraged, Gerty Radnitz got down to business. On her summer vacation in the Austrian Alps, she met a teacher who started her on Latin lessons. That fall, she enrolled at the preparatory school where he taught. A year later, she passed the entrance exams.

At the age of eighteen, Gerty Radnitz began her medical education and met Carl Cori, the man who became her partner in life and in research. Their research into how the body stores and uses sugar and other carbohydrates led to a better understanding of diabetes and other sugar-related diseases. For this, they won the 1947 Nobel Prize for Physiology or Medicine.

Gerty Theresa Radnitz was born on August 15, 1896, in Prague, which was then in the Austro-Hungarian Empire and is now the capital of the Czech Republic. She was the first of three daughters born to Martha and Otto Radnitz. Her father, a successful Jewish chemist, managed sugar refineries. In this turn-of-the-century European world, young women went to finishing schools to prepare for lives as charming, cultured wives and mothers. Gerty, however, who may have been encouraged by her uncle — a pediatrician — pursued a medical career instead.

Gerty met Carl Cori in an anatomy class at the medical school. He was a handsome, shy young man. She was a vivacious, outgoing young woman. Everything about them, from personality to interests, complemented one another. Both loved hiking, skiing, and mountain climbing, and both were sure they wanted to be researchers rather than physicians. They decided to marry. The Cori family, however, opposed the marriage because Gerty was Jewish. Anti-Semitism was strong throughout Europe at that time, and the Coris felt the marriage would hurt Carl's career. To resolve the problem, Gerty converted to Roman Catholicism, Carl's religion. In 1920, following graduation from medical school, they were married.

Although World War I (1914-1918) had been over for almost two years, the European economy was still in a shambles. There were few job opportunities for medical researchers. For a while, Carl worked in the pharmacology department of the University of Graz, and Gerty worked at a children's hospital in Vienna. Realizing they would have to leave Europe to find better medical research opportunities, Carl accepted a job at a cancer center in Buffalo, New York, now known as the Rosewell Park Memorial Institute. He sailed for America in 1922. Six months later, he obtained a post for Gerty as an assistant pathologist and sent for her. In 1927, they became U.S. citizens.

The Coris were very interested in the developing field of biochemistry and the complex processes and reactions that take place in the body. Focusing on the biochemistry of cancerous tumors, they began to investigate how tumors use sugar for energy in order to grow. This work naturally led them to question how normal body tissues store and use sugar. When the Coris began this research, little was known about carbohydrate metabolism (burning sugar for energy). The hormone insulin had recently been discovered and was found to play an important role in controlling the amount of sugar in the blood of diabetics.

The Coris were intrigued with insulin and wondered what role it might play in normal sugar storage and use. To find out, they conducted a series of carefully controlled experiments on laboratory rats. They fed all the rats specified amounts of sugar and then examined what happened to the sugar if the rats were fed insulin. They found that after entering the bloodstream in a form called glucose, some of the sugar was burned for energy, some was converted to fat, but about half was converted to a carbohydrate called glycogen and stored in muscles and the liver. Insulin decreased the amount of sugar stored in the liver.

For six years, the Coris — especially Gerty — analyzed, measured, and ran carefully controlled experiments on laboratory rats. The information they gathered led them to conclude that there is a continuous carbohydrate cycle. Glycogen, stored in muscles and made from excess sugar and starch in the blood, breaks down into glucose, a form of sugar that muscles can use. When the muscles burn glucose, a residue of lactic acid is created. The lactic acid returns through the bloodstream to the liver, where it is converted to glucose. Blood carries this glucose back to the muscle, where it is converted to glycogen and stored until the muscle needs energy. Then it is converted to glucose, and the cycle begins again. By 1929, the Coris had developed the broad outline of this carbohydrate cycle.

Although the science of biochemistry was advancing rapidly in America during the 1920s, the acceptance of women scientists was not. Even though Gerty Cori was in many respects the leader of her husband-wife research team, she was not granted academic recognition for many years. While at the Buffalo cancer center, the Coris together published many papers on carbohydrate metabolism and established their scientific reputations. As a result, job offers began to come in — for Carl but not for Gerty. During one job interview, Gerty Cori was even told that it was "un-American" for a wife to work with her husband. Then, in 1931, Washington University in St. Louis, Missouri, offered jobs to both Coris. Carl became head of the pharmacology department while Gerty was hired merely as a research assistant. In any event, the careers of both Coris flourished in St. Louis. In 1946, Carl became chairman of the biochemistry department, and in 1947 he appointed Gerty as a full professor of biochemistry.

Meanwhile, they continued their sugar metabolism research. They knew that glycogen and glucose underwent biochemical changes as they went through the carbohydrate cycle. What they believed they would find is that enzymes were involved in these biochemical reactions. (Enzymes are special proteins that act as catalysts in living organisms, substances that allow chemical reactions to occur without being involved themselves.) But at that time, very little was known about enzymes.

To study these complex biochemical reactions, the Coris knew they would not be able to use the entire body of a living animal. So they designed an experiment that they could control more precisely. They chopped up some frog muscle, rinsed it with distilled water, and analyzed the biochemicals that remained. What they discovered were new enzymes and a new form of glucose now called *Cori ester*.

While conducting research, Gerty was in charge of the laboratories. She demanded perfection in all experiments, devising methods for purifying the enzymes, hormones, and other biochemicals used in experiments and supervising all aspects of their production. She knew that in the type of biochemical studies they were conducting, any impurity could give a false result, ruining the experiment. In 1936, during the height of her medical experiments, Gerty gave birth to a baby boy. Eventually, he earned a Ph.D. in chemistry and headed a company that supplied biochemicals to medical researchers like the Coris.

In 1939, the Coris made one of their most famous discoveries. They found that an enzyme called phosphorylase is responsible for converting glycogen to glucose and back again. To demonstrate their discovery, Carl mixed Cori ester with phosphorylase in a test tube. This was the first time such a compound had been created outside a living cell.

The Coris worked so closely together on these experiments that colleagues said it was impossible to say which of them was responsible for any particular finding. In the process of studying the complex steps involved in the carbohydrate cycle, the Coris contributed to the understanding and treatment of diabetes as well as to a group of illnesses called glycogen-storage diseases, which are caused by missing enzymes. Their work showed that mistakes in the normal biochemistry of cells are a major factor in a number of diseases. Soon the Cori laboratory at Washington University became a major center for biochemical research. In fact, several Nobel Prize winners were trained in the Cori lab. In 1947, Gerty and Carl themselves were awarded the Nobel Prize for Physiology or Medicine, which they shared with Bernardo Houssay, who made important contributions toward understanding the role of insulin in diabetes.

Although 1947 brought joy, it also brought sadness. Gerty Cori was stricken with a disease. While on a mountain-climbing trip at high altitude, Gerty had fainted. The Coris suspected this signaled that something was wrong with the oxygen-carrying ability of her blood.

Their suspicions were confirmed when medical tests showed that she was suffering from a rare but fatal form of anemia caused by the progressive destruction of her bone marrow.

Gerty Cori lived another ten years with the disease, earning many honors for her work, including a presidential appointment to the board of the newly created National Science Foundation. She continued her research until mid-1957 when she grew too weak to work. Gerty Cori died at home on October 26, 1957. Carl, who remarried, died in 1984 at the age of eighty-eight.

The Coris left an important legacy. They brought biological science right down to the molecular level. Their research proved that genes were involved in many diseases resulting from missing hormones or enzymes. They left future generations the task of finding the exact genetic causes — and perhaps a genetic cure — for the missing enzymes and hormones that they found to be at the root of sugar metabolism diseases.

MARIE SKLODOWSKA CURIE

1867-1934
Nuclear Physicist, Chemist

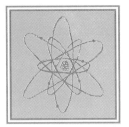

The radium next to Marie Curie's bedside glowed with a cold blue light. In the dark of night, the element she and her husband Pierre had discovered in 1898 had a rare, eerie beauty. Curie knew that radium was highly radioactive. She had coined the term *radioactivity* to describe the mysterious particles given off by certain rare elements. But she didn't believe that the rays could be deadly, even though she suspected that they might be responsible for the ill and tired feeling she had been experiencing ever since she had begun working with the element.

For years, Marie and Pierre Curie had sifted through tons of radioactive uranium ore to isolate radium and polonium, another element. For their work on the nature of radioactivity, the Curies shared the 1903 Nobel Prize for Physics with French physicist Antoine Henri Becquerel. Madame Curie then went on to win the 1911 Nobel Prize for Chemistry for discovering radium. She also became, and remains to this day, the most famous woman scientist in history. Not for another fifty-one years would any other scientist — male or female — win two Nobel Prizes.

Marie Curie was born Marya Sklodowska in Warsaw, Poland, on November 7, 1867. Her early years were marked by great hardship. Her mother, a director of a boarding school for girls, died of tuberculosis when Marya was only four years old. Her widowed father, a physics and math teacher, who was dismissed from job after job for political reasons, could barely support his five children.

At that time, Poland had been divided by Russia and Germany, and Warsaw was under harsh Russian rule. The Russians, believing they could stamp out Polish culture, had been replacing Polish teachers with Russian ones. But, instead, a great Polish nationalist movement took root, and education of Polish men and women became one of its strongest tenets. Marya and her sister Bronya, believing education was a patriotic duty, made a pact together. They decided that Bronya would study medicine at the University of Paris and Marya would support her. Then Bronya would bring Marya to Paris. To fulfill her end of the pact, Marya worked as a governess in Poland for six years but also continued her private studies in chemistry and mathematics.

Then in 1891, Marya went to France. She enrolled at the University of Paris, changed her name to Marie, and rented a tiny sixth-floor room where she immersed herself in her studies, surviving most of the time on only bread and hot chocolate. In 1894, after having earned degrees in physics and mathematics, she met Pierre Curie. They fell in love and were married in a simple civil ceremony the following year. For their honeymoon, they took a bicycle tour — a sport they would enjoy throughout their married life.

During the next two years, Pierre obtained a professorship at a science college, Marie studied for a teaching certificate, and their first child, Irene, was born. Then in 1896, Marie began work on her doctorate. For her thesis, she chose to explore the results of an experiment on X rays conducted by the French physicist Antoine Henri Becquerel. Becquerel had been fascinated by the newly discovered X rays that emanated from cathode-ray tubes. He wondered if X rays were given off by other objects, such as fluorescent crystals, which give off light after being exposed to rays such as sunlight. X rays from cathode-ray tubes made foggy images on photographic plates. So Becquerel hypothesized that if fluorescent crystals give off X rays, they too would fog photographic plates. To test this theory, Becquerel wrapped photographic plates in heavy black paper so that no sunlight could penetrate. Then he placed a piece of fluorescent material on top of the paper and set it all on a windowsill. But the weather turned cloudy, so Becquerel put the paper-wrapped plates and the fluorescent crystal in a drawer. A few days later, he developed the photographic plates anyway and discovered foggy images all over them. Rays were coming from the crystals, he concluded, and specifically from small amounts of uranium in the crystals. He found that any substance containing uranium gave off this radiation. He also found that uranium causes the air around it to conduct electricity.

To explore this phenomenon, Marie used a device her husband had invented to detect electric charges around mineral samples. She found that another element, thorium, also gave off radiation. She named this process of spontaneous radiation, radioactivity. Next, she measured the strength of electric current around uranium/thorium ore samples and concluded that the radioactivity must be coming from the atom itself. She also found that pitchblende, a uranium ore, was about three times as radioactive as uranium, and thus must contain at least one more radioactive element.

At this point, Pierre decided to join his wife in her search for the new radioactive element. By chemically separating elements from the uranium ore and measuring their radioactivity, the Curies discovered an element that was 400 times more radioactive than uranium. Madame Curie named it polonium for her native Poland. She continued to work with a polonium sample, and discovered another element. This element, which was a million times more radioactive than uranium, she named radium.

Next on their agenda was the isolation of pure samples of these new elements for study. Because only tiny amounts of polonium and radium could be detected in the uranium ore samples, the Curies knew they would have to sift through tons of pitchblende to gather even small quantities of the new elements. They located an abandoned storage shed at Pierre's college that would provide sufficient space for this undertaking and began to work. Over time, the miserable little shed with leaky roof and poor ventilation, which was stifling hot in summer and freezing cold in winter, became part of the Curie legend. Under wretched conditions, between 1898 and 1902, the Curies sifted through tons of uranium ore to isolate only one-tenth gram of the pure radium chloride salt. During the process, they breathed in hazardous radon gas and handled material giving off rays that damaged their skin and bone marrow. They suspected that the radioactivity was taking a toll on their health, but they had no idea how dangerous these substances really were.

After radium was isolated, both wonderful and trivial applications were developed for the cold blue light — everything from shrinking the tumors of cancer patients to making the faces of clocks glow in the dark. Had the Curies patented their radium-extraction process, they would have become millionaires. But they did not believe this was an ethical thing to do. Pierre and Marie considered themselves leftist liberals. They thought that government should work to improve the lives of ordinary people and that science should be kept apart from commercial applications.

The scientific world immediately recognized the importance of the Curies' discoveries and awarded them and Becquerel the 1903 Nobel Prize in Physics for their work on Becquerel's radiation discovery. Unfortunately, both Pierre and Marie were too sick from what we now know as radiation poisoning to travel to Sweden and accept the prize.

In 1904, a professorship in physics was created for Pierre at the Sorbonne, the liberal arts and sciences college of the University of Paris. With this new position, the economic lives of the Curies improved. But two years later, everything changed. On April 19, 1906, Pierre Curie was run over by a horsedrawn wagon and killed instantly. Overnight, Madame Curie became a widow and a single parent with two daughters to raise: Irene, who would become a Nobel Prize-winning physicist, and Eve, who would write a famous biography of her mother.

In carrying out her public duties after Pierre's death, Marie's demeanor was sad but calm. Privately, she was near collapse. She began writing letters to Pierre in a private diary, a practice she continued for years. Gradually, she adjusted to her circumstances. The University of Paris gave her a paid position as a lecturer in physics. In 1908, she took over the professorship formerly held by her husband, thus becoming the first woman professor in the history of the university. Although she loved her research work, she was never comfortable giving lectures. To her daughters, she appeared to undergo a personality change whenever she had to lecture or appear before large groups of people. To visiting strangers, the most famous woman scientist in the world seemed oddly timid. Social life in the Curie household diminished to almost nothing.

Then in 1911, Madame Curie was swept up in two public scandals created by the same French press that had previously portrayed her as a saint of science. The first involved her bid

for election to the prestigious French Academy of Sciences. Already up for election was an elderly scientist who happened to be a devout Catholic. His supporters began a campaign that portrayed Curie as anti-Semitic and a foreigner supported by liberals, feminists, and anti-Church groups. To liberals, she was portrayed as a Catholic. As a result of the bad publicity, Curie lost her bid for election by one vote. (Not until 1979 did the French Academy of Sciences elect a woman member.)

The second scandal involved an alleged love affair with a married Frenchman. It is not clear what Marie Curie's involvement was, but certain newspapers portrayed her as a Polish foreigner who was stealing the husband of a loyal, honest Frenchwoman. The scandal reverberated throughout the University of Paris and even the French government.

In 1911, on the verge of a nervous collapse, Madame Curie reportedly received the news that she had been nominated for the Nobel Prize in Chemistry for the discovery of radium. In describing the epic work for which she was given the Nobel Prize and how it changed the nature of chemistry and physics, Madame Curie had this to say: "We are now used to working with substances which manifest their presence to us only by their radioactive properties. . . . This is a particular kind of chemistry . . . which could well be called the chemistry of the imponderable."

At the outbreak of World War I in Europe (1914-1918), Madam Curie performed yet another great service to the world. Realizing that X rays could be used to locate broken bones, bullets, and pieces of shrapnel in wounded soldiers on the front lines, she organized mobile X-ray units for the French Army medical corps, set up more than 200 battlefield X-ray units, and trained 150 women to operate them. After the war, she became director of the newly established French Radium Institute, a place where scientists could do research and doctors could experiment with medical applications for radiation. But because the war had left France economically destitute, there was no money for equipment or supplies. And Curie had less than one gram of radium to work with.

Through the efforts of an American journalist, a campaign was launched in the 1920s for the women of the United States to buy radium for Marie Curie. As part of this fund-raising effort, she and her daughters made two visits to America where, in her trademark black cotton dress, she was greeted by adoring crowds. The campaign raised enough money to purchase a gram of radium.

For the remainder of her life, Madame Curie served as fund-raiser and administrator for her Radium Institute. Eventually, her daughter Irene would carry out Nobel Prize-winning research there, too. But now, all was not well at the institute. By the mid-1920s, several workers had died of cancer. Elsewhere in the world, doctors were turning up evidence that radioactivity was the cause. Unwilling to accept the truth, Marie Curie blamed the working conditions on workers failing to get enough fresh air. Tragically, the Radium Institute under her leadership never investigated the health hazards of radiation.

Eventually, the massive amounts of radiation to which Madame Curie had been exposed took its toll. Having suffered from chronic exhaustion all of her professional life, she was now almost blinded by radiation-caused cataracts. On July 4, 1934, Marie Curie died of leukemia, undoubtedly brought on by the radiation to which she had devoted her life.

ELLA CARA DELORIA

1889-1971
Anthropologist, Linguist

 A terrible blizzard was raging on the Yankton Sioux Reservation in South Dakota on the day Ella Cara Deloria was born. This inspired her Sioux name — *Anpetu Waste Win*, meaning "Beautiful Day Woman." To those who knew her later in life, this name reflected the kind and gracious nature of the woman anthropologist who carefully studied and then created the fullest account of the culture, language, and traditions of the Dakota people.

Ella Cara Deloria was born in 1889, near the town of Lake Andes, South Dakota. She was the eldest of four children born to Philip Deloria, the first Native American Episcopal priest, and Mary Sully Bordeau Deloria, the granddaughter of Irish artist Thomas Sully. Ella Deloria lived on the Standing Rock Reservation and attended St. Elizabeth's mission school until she was fourteen years old. She then enrolled in All Saints School in Sioux Falls, South Dakota. She began her college education at the University of Chicago in 1910, transferred to Oberlin College in Ohio in 1911, and then went to Teacher's College at Columbia University in New York City, where she graduated in 1915. At Columbia she became acquainted with the distinguished anthropologist Franz Boas, who would have a great influence on her life.

From 1915 to 1919, Ella Deloria taught at All Saints Episcopal High School in Sioux Falls. She then undertook a project for the Young Women's Christian Association that proved the benefits of physical education for Native American girls. In 1923, she went to Lawrence, Kansas, to teach physical education at the Haskell Indian School, all the while harboring a deep desire to research the traditional language and culture of the Dakota.

In 1927, after being asked by Franz Boas to teach American Indian dialects to anthropology students at Columbia, Deloria resigned from Haskell and embarked on a career as an anthropologic linguist. She worked with Boas on Dakota research, publishing scholarly works with him until his death in 1942. Using Boas's techniques, she traveled extensively, visiting

Dakota and Lakota reservations to interview elders and gather information about their language, beliefs, and lifestyle. She also edited and translated written texts. Regularly she sent her research to Franz Boas or to Ruth Benedict, a colleague. Deloria's work resulted in several books: *Dakota Texts* (1932), which documented Native American myths and stories; *Dakota Grammar* (1941), which she coauthored with Boas; and *Speaking of Indians*, an account of Dakota life, which she wrote and her sister Mary illustrated. She also wrote *Waterlily*, a novel that focused on Indian life from a woman's point of view, although the book was not published until long after her death.

Deloria's years of research were difficult. She existed mainly on small grants and fees from writing and speaking engagements. Honoring family obligations often made it difficult for her to continue her research. However, while taking care of her father, her sister, and her nephews, she still managed to record substantial information about Dakota life and produce a definitive dictionary and grammar. By the 1940s, she was a recognized authority on their language and culture.

In 1955, Deloria became director of St. Elizabeth's mission school, a post she held until 1958. She then spent a brief time working for the Sioux Indian Museum in Rapid City, South Dakota, and serving as assistant director of the W. H. Over Museum at the University of South Dakota. Ella Deloria was working on a Lakota Sioux dictionary shortly before her death on February 12, 1971.

ALICE EASTWOOD

1859-1953
Botanist

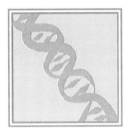

The shaking of her bed awakened Alice Eastwood on the morning of April 18, 1906. By the time she dressed and went outside, smoke was hanging heavy over the city of San Francisco. A great earthquake had ruptured gas lines and reduced blocks of buildings to rubble. Fire was spreading everywhere and would soon consume four square miles of San Francisco, including the California Academy of Sciences on Market Street where Eastwood had spent more than twelve years building an extensive collection of California plants. She rushed to the academy, and with a friend, broke through the locked front door. The stairs to her sixth-floor office were gone, shaken loose by the earthquake, but the handrail was still firmly attached to the wall. Using this and fragments of stairs, Eastwood climbed up to her office and rescued almost 1,500 rare plant specimens, which she had earlier separated from the main collection in the herbarium. With the specimens wrapped in a large work apron, she escaped just before flames consumed the building.

Eastwood was not one to let trouble get her down. In a letter to *Science* magazine, describing her experience, she said, "My own destroyed work I do not lament, for it was a joy to me while I did it, and I can still have the same joy in starting it again. . . ." And start again she did. This self-educated frontier botanist created an even better collection of plants at the new California Academy of Sciences and thus ensured her own reputation as one of the greatest botanists in the world.

Alice Eastwood was born on January 19, 1859, in Toronto, Canada. Her childhood was an unsettling one. Her parents, Colin and Eliza Jane, had emigrated from Ireland, and the family lived on the grounds of the Toronto Asylum for the Insane, where her father worked.

When Alice was six years old, her mother died. Her father went off to try his hand at storekeeping and left Alice and her brother and sister in Canada with their Uncle William, a physician. In her uncle's home, Alice's lifelong informal education as a botanist took root.

She carefully observed each of the plants on her uncle's country estate and learned their difficult Latin names. When she and her sister were sent to school at a nearby convent, Alice learned about gardening.

Several years later, Alice's father settled in Denver, Colorado, built a house, and brought the family back together again. Alice, now a teenager, attended the new East Denver High School. Because the family was still very poor, Alice had to work as a housekeeper, nursemaid, and even in a hat factory. She was twenty years old when she finally graduated from high school in 1879, the valedictorian of her class. After graduation, she accepted a teaching position at East Denver High School.

Although Eastwood never attended college, she continued to educate herself, especially about botany. She loved to collect plants. During the summer months, she traveled to the most remote parts of the Rocky Mountains in search of unusual plants. As a result, she amassed a large variety of Colorado plant specimens, which eventually formed the core of the University of Colorado's Herbarium.

Because of good investments in Denver real estate that she and her father had made over the years, Alice Eastwood was able to quit her teaching job and continue traveling. In 1890, she visited the California Academy of Sciences in San Francisco, where she met Katharine Brandegee, the curator of botany, and her husband, a biologist. In 1892, they invited her to join them at the academy as an assistant curator. The following year, when the Brandegees retired, Eastwood took over as curator of botany and editor of the academy's botany journal. Under her guidance, the California botany collection grew — until the tragic earthquake and fire of 1906.

The California Academy was not rebuilt until 1912. During those six years, Alice Eastwood meticulously studied the plant collections at the Smithsonian Institution in Washington, D.C., the New York Botanical Garden, and public gardens in London and Paris. When she returned to San Francisco, she expanded the academy's botany collection to more than 340,000 specimens. She was also active in encouraging the efforts of amateur botanists and gardeners and in educating the public about the need to save California's native plants, especially the giant redwoods.

Although she had no formal higher education, Alice Eastwood gained recognition from the scientific community. She was the only woman with the star for distinction next to her name in every volume of *American Men of Science* published during her lifetime. In 1950, at the age of ninety-two, Alice Eastwood flew to Stockholm, Sweden, to serve as honorary president of the Seventh International Botanical Congress. She remained active until her death from cancer on October 30, 1953.

TILLY EDINGER

1897-1967
Paleontologist

 To avoid drawing attention to herself, the Jewish director of the Senckenberg Museum in Frankfurt, Germany, removed her name from the office door. When she came to work, she slipped in through a side entrance. As a Jew living in Nazi Germany in the 1930s, Tilly Edinger knew such precautions were necessary if she were to survive the discriminatory laws denying Jews employment. Insisting on continuing her research on fossil brains, Endinger remained at the Frankfurt museum until threats of personal danger encouraged her to escape to America. There she continued her research, eventually proving that evolution does not occur in a straight line with one species neatly leading to another, but that species branch, with some branches coming to a dead end and others leading to living species.

Johanna Gabrielle Ottelie Edinger was born in Frankfurt am Main on November 13, 1897. Her parents were wealthy and prominent in Frankfurt society. Her father, a medical researcher, was founder of the new field of comparative neurology, which compared and contrasted features of the brain and nervous system in various species. Her mother was concerned with the plight of the poor and with bringing about social reform. For their contributions to the city of Frankfurt, a street was named in her father's honor, and a bust of her mother graced the town park.

The Edinger children lived a life of privilege. Although money was not an issue when it came to education, the type of education certainly was. Tilly's father did not approve of young women entering certain professions. Nevertheless, he did not stop his daughter Tilly from getting a university education. Her first choice was geology. But when she discovered that there were few opportunities in Europe for women in this field, she turned to the related science of paleontology, which studies fossil remains of prehistoric plants and animals.

Tilly Edinger studied at the universities of Heidelberg and Munich and received a Ph.D. from the University of Frankfurt in 1921. After receiving her doctorate, she remained at the university as an assistant in paleontology. Then in 1927, she became curator of the vertebrate fossil collection at the Senckenberg Museum. Although the position allowed her to publish the results of her research, she received no payment because she was a woman.

At the time, Edinger's interest focused on the study of fossil brains. This type of study is difficult because no actual fossil brains exist. When an animal dies, organs and other soft tissue, such as the brain, decay and disappear. But hard tissue, such as bone, which does not decay as quickly and may be preserved by minerals, can be studied. In living mammals, the brain fills the entire cavity inside the skull, pressing tightly against the bone. The brain, therefore, makes an impression of itself inside the skull. Edinger knew that by filling the brain cavity inside a fossil skull with plaster or some other material, she could create a likeness of a creature's brain. Because she was the

first scientist to use this technique to make brain casts of various prehistoric creatures and compare them, she is considered to be the founder of the field of paleoneurology — the study of fossil brains. Her first major work, published in 1929, was called *Fossil Brains*.

By 1933, Germany and Tilly Edinger's life were in the process of change. Adolf Hitler and the Nazi Party, then in control of Germany, were purging Jews from positions of power in the country. Their edict, which made it illegal to employ Jews, jeopardized the work and safety of many people, including Tilly Edinger. To protect her and her work, friends at the museum managed to keep her position secret for five years. But in 1938, realizing she was in mortal danger, Edinger fled to London and then to the United States. Her brother Fritz, who was not so lucky, died later in a Nazi concentration camp.

In the United States, Edinger found a post at Harvard University's Museum of Comparative Zoology, where she worked for the rest of her life. She took one year off to teach at Wellesley College in Massachusetts. In 1948, she published her second major work, *The Evolution of the Horse Brain*, which offered proof that a large forebrain, a mark of intelligence, evolved a number of times in different mammals. This finding discredited the "chain of being" theory, which proposed that evolution progressed from lower to higher animals in a straight line.

Tilly Edinger's work inspired other paleontologists to use fossil brains to trace the history of evolution. Unfortunately her life and research were cut short by an accident in 1967. While walking near her home in Cambridge, Massachussetts, she was struck by a car and fatally injured. She died on May 27, 1967.

GERTRUDE BELLE ELION

1918-
Biochemist

The stock market crash of 1929 changed the course of Trudy Elion's life. Like many other families, Trudy's parents lost a fortune. As a result, her plans for the future changed. She had to work her way through college and never did complete her doctorate. Elion had a special kind of perseverance. She became a biochemical researcher in the pharmaceutical industry and developed some of the most revolutionary drugs of the twentieth century: chemotherapy for leukemia, a drug for gout, a drug that made organ transplants possible, and acyclovir for treating herpesvirus infections. And her drug development methods were used to synthesize AZT, the first drug for treating AIDS. For her contribution to understanding the metabolism of the natural compounds on which these drugs were based, Gertrude Elion shared the 1988 Nobel Prize for Physiology or Medicine with her mentor and research partner George H. Hitchings and with Sir James W. Black, who developed the first beta-blocker drug.

Gertrude Belle Elion was born on January 23, 1918, in New York City. Both of her parents were immigrants. Her father, Robert, came from Lithuania, and her mother, Bertha Cohen, from Poland, which was then part of Russia. Both parents belonged to Jewish families with a long, scholarly tradition. Robert, like many European immigrants in the early 1900s, was determined to make good in America. He worked his way through school to become a dentist, then invested a portion of what he earned in stocks and real estate. Bertha went to night school to learn English and worked as a seamstress until she married Robert at age nineteen. Gertrude's father did very well financially. Until the crash of 1929 forced him into bankruptcy.

Gertrude Elion graduated from high school at age fifteen and attended Hunter College, the women's college of the City University of New York, where tuition was free. She graduated in 1937 with a degree in chemistry and highest honors. She wanted to continue her education in graduate school but lacked the money. The death of her beloved grandfather from stomach cancer had made her determined to do cancer research. Immediately she applied for fellowships. Time and again her applications were turned down because she was a woman. After fifteen tries, she gave up and enrolled in secretarial school instead. Her stay in secretarial school lasted only six weeks, until she got her first job.

For seven years, Elion worked in various jobs, taught biochemistry to nursing students, and assisted in a chemistry lab for $20 a week. When she had saved a year's tuition, she enrolled as a graduate student in the chemistry department at New York University, while continuing to work nights and weekends. It was during this time that she met Leonard, the great love of her life, and decided to marry him. Her decision would hold bittersweet memories for the rest of her life. Leonard was studying to be a statistician, but after returning from a fellowship abroad, he was stricken by a bacterial infection of the heart valves and lining. This occurred in the days before antibiotics were discovered, and Leonard died. Elion, heartbroken, never married.

In 1942, as more men were called to serve in World War II (1939-1945), civilian jobs were filled by women. When job opportunities in laboratories began opening up, Elion took a job with the A&P food chain checking the quality of ingredients in food products. Her second job was with Johnson & Johnson laboratories. Then almost by accident, she found the drug company that became her employer for life.

Elion's father happened to receive a sample of Empirin painkillers at his dental office from the Burroughs Wellcome Company in Tuckahoe, New York. He suggested that Gertrude call the company to inquire if they were hiring. Shortly after calling Burroughs, she was hired as the laboratory assistant to George Hitchings. He was working out a new way to develop drugs by imitating natural compounds, instead of the usual trial-and-error methods. Hitchings theorized that it should be possible to synthesize artificial compounds that were similar to the natural ones that cells needed for growth. By fooling certain cells into taking in these compounds, Hitchings believed that harmful or defective cells or organisms would be killed. As a result, it should be possible to block the growth of cancer cells with this technique. His idea was to develop false building blocks that cancerous cells would use when replicating. The false building blocks would destroy the cancerous cells without harming normal cells.

Hitchings assigned Elion to work with some of these building blocks, a group of nucleic acid bases called purines. Two purines, adenine and guanine, are basic parts of the DNA molecule. (DNA is the nucleic acid of which genes are formed, and genes control all the functions of a cell.) So Elion went to work on synthesizing compounds that would interfere with nucleic acids essential for the growth of cancer cells. In 1950, she developed two anticancer drugs, thioguanine and 6-MP.

Until 6-MP was developed, childhood leukemia, a cancer of the blood-forming tissues, was almost always fatal. In early treatment with 6-MP, the stricken children initially improved, but then relapsed and died. Also, 6-MP had serious side effects, including nausea and vomiting. When Elion visited the children being treated with her drug, her research took on a powerful emotional urgency. She felt more like a doctor than a laboratory chemist. Eventually, Elion and other researchers learned that 6-MP in combination with other anticancer drugs could cure childhood leukemia.

Meanwhile, Elion had been analyzing what happens to 6-MP in the body, hoping to prolong the drug's cancer-killing effects. She never solved that problem, but she and other scientists found that 6-MP and closely related compounds had other revolutionary uses. In 1958, scientists discovered that 6-MP could suppress the immune system and wondered if it could be used in organ transplant operations. (The job of the immune system is to seek out and destroy anything foreign invading the body. This includes organ transplants as well as bacteria and viruses. As a result, the immune system normally rejects any grafted tissue.)

Hitchings and Elion, working with a surgeon, developed a drug called Imuran, which suppresses the immune system, making organ transplants possible. In 1961, the first successful human kidney transplant from an unrelated donor was performed. Since then, many kidney transplant patients have owed their survival to Elion's Imuran.

Elion made another discovery about 6-MP that led to a treatment for gout. While trying to extend the effectiveness of 6-MP against cancer cells, she found that a particular enzyme in the body breaks down 6-MP. Other Burroughs Wellcome chemists created a compound that blocks the action of that enzyme. Elion discovered that the compound allopurinol also prevents the build-up of uric acid, a condition that causes the severe pain of gout.

In 1968, after becoming head of the department of experimental therapy, Elion turned her attention to viruses. (Unlike bacteria, viruses cannot be killed by antibiotics.) She put her team to work on a drug treatment for herpesvirus infections. These viruses are responsible for chicken pox, shingles, cold sores, and genital sores. Elion and her team developed acyclovir, a compound similar to one the virus needs to reproduce itself. The drug does not harm other cells, but when the virus takes it in, an enzyme turns acyclovir into a form that destroys the virus. Elion began working with acyclovir in 1974, and seven years later, it won FDA approval to be marketed as Zovirax.

Elion retired from Burroughs Wellcome in 1983. By that time, the company had moved to Research Triangle Park in North Carolina and Elion had moved to a town house in Chapel Hill. But hers was an active retirement. She served as a consultant to the drug company, on the advisory committees of the World Health Organization, on the National Cancer Advisory Board, and as a research professor at Duke University. She also continued to pursue her life-long interests — performances by New York's Metropolitan Opera and travel to exotic lands.

During her noteworthy career, Gertrude Belle Elion collected an impressive array of awards and honors, including honorary doctorates, the National Medal of Science, and election to the National Academy of Sciences. For her, winning the 1988 Nobel Prize for Physiology or Medicine was, indeed, the capstone of her career. However, it was just the icing on the cake. Watching people get well as a result of the drugs she has developed, is for her, the greatest reward.

Williamina Paton Stevens Fleming

1857-1911
Astronomer

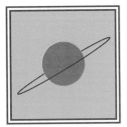

As a young woman, the life of Williamina Fleming did not look promising. At the age of twenty-two, she found herself in a strange new country, pregnant, and without the support of a husband. To survive, she had to take a job as a maid. But Fleming was a very intelligent woman, and by taking advantage of a unique set of opportunities that came her way, she learned the science of astronomy, mastered a new photographic technique for studying stars, and became the most famous woman astronomer of her time in America. As a measure of how far she rose in the world of science, this single working mother had the distinction of being the first woman appointed to an official position at Harvard by the university's governing board.

Williamina Paton Stevens was born on May 15, 1857, in Dundee, Scotland. Her father was a tradesman with a carving and gilding business. He died when she was seven years old, and she was cared for by her mother's family. Williamina was educated at Dundee public schools and must have been a brilliant student, because at the age of fourteen, she became a "pupil-teacher." For the next five years, she taught school, until she married James Orr Fleming in 1877.

The young couple, like so many others at that time, decided to seek their fortune in America. So in 1878, they left Scotland and settled in Boston, Massachusetts. But things did not go well for them personally, and the following year, the marriage broke up. By that time, Fleming was pregnant, and had no one to rely on for support but herself. She sought employment in one of the few jobs open to women at the time — as a maid or housekeeper. As fate would have it, she was hired to work in the household of Edward C. Pickering, director of the Harvard Astronomical Observatory. She so admired Professor Pickering that when her son was born she named him Edward Pickering Fleming.

Pickering was involved in photographing the spectra of light emitted, or given off, by various stars. The fact that sunlight is made up of a spectrum of colors was discovered in the 1600s by English physicist Sir Isaac Newton. He noticed that light breaks up into the various colors of the rainbow, or visible spectrum, when it passes through a prism. In the 1800s, scientists learned that when light passes through a slit and then a prism, the spectrum spreads out to reveal a pattern of lines, or bands. They then learned that each chemical element, when heated, gives off a distinctive pattern of these bands. No two bands are alike, just as no two sets of fingerprints are alike. By analyzing the pattern of lights, scientists realized that they could learn what elements stars contain. (Instruments for doing this are called spectroscopes, and the photographic images they produce are called spectrograms.)

Williamina Fleming's opportunity to work with spectrograms at the Harvard Observatory came about when Pickering, displeased with the work of a male assistant, jokingly said that even his Scottish maid could do a better job. Fleming went to work, first as a clerk and a computer (one who computes or calculates), then as an astronomer analyzing photographic plates of the spectra of thousands of stars. In the process, she discovered 222 variable stars (stars that vary in brightness) and 10 novas (stars that suddenly grow bright because their outer layers have exploded). She developed a system for classifying stars according to their spectra and in 1890 published a catalog of more than 10,000 stars. In 1898, the Harvard Corporation officially named her curator of astronomical photographs.

Williamina Paton Stevens Fleming was awarded many honors by institutions in the United States, France, and Mexico. In 1906, she became the first American woman elected to Great Britain's Royal Astronomical Society. She died of pneumonia on May 21, 1911.

Dian Fossey

1932-1985
Zoologist

When Goldie died, young Dian Fossey was grief-stricken. Goldie was her favorite goldfish, and it had been around for six years. Although goldfish were the only animals Dian's parents would allow her to keep, Dian loved all animals. When she grew up, she made them her life's work. After visiting Africa in 1963, Dian was determined to return to study the rare mountain gorillas in Congo. Eventually, she fought tirelessly to preserve the habitat of gorillas, sometimes using tactics that other people thought were too extreme. Her controversial efforts to save the mountain gorillas from extinction may have led to her death.

Dian Fossey was born on January 16, 1932, in San Francisco, California. She began college with the idea of becoming a veterinarian, but then switched to occupational therapy. After graduating from San Jose State College in 1954, and completing clinical training in 1956, she moved to Louisville, Kentucky, to direct the occupational therapy department at the Kosair Crippled Children's Hospital. Although she had a rewarding career and an exciting hobby — horseback riding — she felt there was something important missing from her life.

Fossey had become fascinated with the mountain gorillas that lived in a volcanic mountain range in Africa. "I had this great urge, this need to go to Africa," she once told a newspaper reporter. "I had it the day I was born. Some may call it destiny. My parents and friends called it dismaying."

No matter what her parents and friends thought, Fossey acted on her beliefs. She knew that if she was to see Africa and the mountain gorillas she had better make some plans. She borrowed $8,000 and arranged to take a seven-week African safari in 1963. What began as a vacation would shape the remainder of her life.

Her safari included a stop at Tanzania's Olduvai Gorge, where Mary and Louis Leakey, British anthropologists, were unearthing fossils of prehuman ancestors. Upon meeting the

Leakeys, Fossey expressed her fascination with the mountain gorillas and her desire to see them. Just how powerful this desire was became apparent when Fossey fell at the Olduvai excavation site and broke her ankle. Not allowing this to stop her, she hobbled off to Congo (now called Zaire) two weeks later, for her first glimpse of a jet-black mountain gorilla.

When the safari was over, Fossey had to return to her job in Louisville. But she had made an impression on Louis Leakey, who was looking for people to observe ape behavior as part of a research study. Leakey believed that there was a connection between ape behavior and the behavior of the ancient beings whose fossil remains he and his wife were uncovering. He already had Jane Goodall observing chimpanzees in Tanzania. Having Dian Fossey observing mountain gorillas in Rwanda, Congo, and Uganda would add to his research. So in 1966, Leakey visited Fossey in Louisville and arranged for her to set up a long-term program for observing mountain gorillas.

By the end of 1966, Fossey was in Africa. She began to study observing and data-collecting techniques with Goodall at the Gombe chimpanzee reserve in Tanzania before purchasing camping equipment for her own research station in a Congo national park. By early 1967, she had set up her own camp and was facing her first challenge — to win the acceptance of the gorillas. After months of imitating their behavior, such as walking on her knuckles and pretending to eat gorilla food, the gorillas allowed her to get close enough to carry out her observations.

Her next challenge was to deal with the political situation. The gorillas' territory covered remote volcanic mountain ranges in parts of Congo, Rwanda, and Uganda. At that time, there was a great deal of political turmoil in those countries, as they sought to gain independence from European colonial rule. After only seven months of observing gorillas, Fossey was arrested by Congolese authorities who were suspicious of her activities. She managed to escape to Uganda and then set up an observing post, the Karisoke Research Center, in the mountains of Rwanda. She preferred to do her observing alone, aided only by native African trackers and helpers. The Africans named her *Nyiramacibili*, the "Lady Who Lives Alone in the Forest."

As a result of her patient observations, Fossey learned that gorillas live in stable family units headed by a dominant male. She called these large black males silverbacks. Because each gorilla had a unique personality, she gave them individual names. Her favorite silverback she called Digit. As she studied gorilla family life, Fossey learned that adult gorillas fight fiercely to protect an infant in a family group, and that group members care for each other when injured or sick. Although she uncovered instances of infanticide and cannibalism among them, they were a peaceful species — not at all like the King Kong stereotype in the movies. Fossey called them "gentle giants."

In the early 1970s, Fossey left Africa to study for her Ph.D. in zoology at Cambridge University in England. She was awarded her doctorate in 1974, and then returned to the research center in Rwanda. Although Fossey always preferred to work and live alone, she reluctantly accepted assistance from student volunteers from time to time. Few stayed very long in the primitive and isolated research camp, but those who did helped carry out a census of the mountain gorilla population.

Fossey's gorilla census showed that their numbers were dropping rapidly, from more than 480 in the early 1960s to about 240 by 1981. There were a number of reasons for the decline. First, the Rwandan population was growing, and impoverished families needed farmland to support themselves. The government gave up some of the parkland for agriculture, thus destroying the mountain gorillas' habitat. Second, gorillas were being caught in poachers' traps set for other animals. And sometimes poachers or hunters illegally killed the gorillas for trophies. Also, gorillas were being captured for shipment to zoos. When a baby gorilla was captured, the adults would fight to their death to save the baby.

In 1978, when Digit was killed by poachers, Fossey began an urgent and frenetic campaign to tell the world about the plight of the mountain gorillas. She established the Digit Fund to raise money for equipping patrols against poachers. She also participated in making several television programs about gorillas. But her intense lifestyle began taking its toll. In 1980, in ill health, Fossey returned to the United States. A lack of calcium in her diet had weakened her bones and rotted her teeth. While on the mend, Fossey taught at Cornell University in Ithaca, New York. In 1982, she finished writing her popular book, *Gorillas in the Mist*, which described her research and told how the very existence of gorillas was being threatened by human activity.

Upon returning to Africa, Fossey took up the cause of the gorillas with renewed enthusiasm. This time she was challenged on many fronts. There were game poachers; the Rwandan government, who wanted more land for agriculture; local game wardens, who did not enforce anti-poaching laws; and poor farmers, who needed land on which to graze cattle and grow crops. Faced with such opposition, Fossey grew increasingly more militant in her efforts to protect the gorillas. Some people criticized her tactics, which were earning her powerful enemies.

The story of Dian Fossey and the mountain gorillas reached its conclusion on December 27, 1985, when Dian was found murdered in her cabin. Sometime during the night, an assassin had broken in and hacked her to death with a large machete-like knife. The Rwandan government accused her research assistant, Wayne R. McGuire, who had left Rwanda before his trial and conviction. Many observers doubted his guilt, however, and instead thought she was killed by poachers who were angered by her interference with their gorilla trade. Sadly, the crime has never been solved to the satisfaction of everyone.

In 1988, a motion picture, *Gorillas in the Mist*, was made of Dian Fossey's life and death. Fossey is buried at the Karisoke Research Station next to the graves of many of her slain gorillas. On her tombstone is the inscription, NYIRAMACIBILI — the "Lady Who Lives Alone in the Forest."

ROSALIND ELSIE FRANKLIN

1920-1958
X-Ray Crystallographer, Molecular Biologist

Even in the scientific community, stories about professional jealousy and destructive personal disagreements surface. One such story involved the brilliant young X-ray crystallographer Rosalind Franklin and the discovery of the structure of DNA, the master molecule of life. Over the years, science historians have uncovered evidence that might suggest American molecular biologist James Watson and British biologist Francis Crick, who claimed credit for the discovery of the DNA structure, may have used Franklin's DNA data without her knowledge. Also, some critics say that Watson and Crick failed to give Franklin proper credit for her role in the discovery of some of the greatest scientific information of the twentieth century. For the discovery of DNA's structure, Watson and Crick shared the 1962 Nobel Prize for Physiology or Medicine with British biophysicist Maurice Wilkins. Franklin, who had died four years earlier at the age of thirty-seven, was never mentioned. Since then, however, her role in this great discovery has become much clearer.

Rosalind Elsie Franklin was born on July 25, 1920, in London, England. Her father, a wealthy banker, and her mother and the five Franklin children enjoyed a privileged lifestyle complete with large homes in London and the English countryside and a staff of servants to maintain them. Even as a young girl, Rosalind did not enjoy the approved activities for girls of that time. She disliked playing with dolls and much preferred building things. And according to her mother, she was much too literal minded.

While attending St. Paul Girls' School in London, Rosalind developed an interest in science — first in astronomy, then in physics and chemistry. She passed the entrance examination at Cambridge University and was accepted. But her father was firmly against university education for women. He thought wealthy young women should do volunteer work. So he refused to pay her tuition.

Rosalind's extended family, however, had a long tradition of social activism and support for women's rights, as did many other liberal Jewish families. When one of her aunts offered to pay Rosalind's tuition, Rosalind's mother also came to her support, eventually forcing her father to give in. But he never liked the idea, and Rosalind never forgave his opposition to her education.

In 1938, Rosalind Franklin enrolled at Cambridge University. She graduated in 1941. With World War II (1939-1945) underway, she took a job with a British government agency that was researching ways of using coal supplies more efficiently. At that time, German planes were flying frequent bombing raids over London, and Franklin had to ride her bicycle over a vast exposed area in order to get to her laboratory.

While conducting research for the agency, she made important discoveries about the molecular structure of coal and carbon, which were later used to develop strong carbon fiber materials and to slow reactions in nuclear power plants. Ultimately, her research formed the basis of her Ph.D. dissertation and she received her doctorate in 1945.

From 1947 to 1950, Franklin lived in Paris, France, where she turned her attention to the branch of physics called X-ray crystallography. The branch was developed in the early 1900s by a father-and-son team — British physicists Sir William Henry Bragg and Sir William Lawrence Bragg. In this technique, a beam of X rays is sent through a crystal, and when the X-rays strike atoms in the crystal, they bounce off at an angle and make an image on photographic film. By studying the images on film, X-ray crystallographers can determine how the atoms are arranged.

In 1951, Franklin returned to London, where she accepted a position at Kings College. There, research scientists were studying living cells and making X-ray images of DNA molecules. They knew that DNA somehow passes the genetic code from one generation to another, but they had no idea how. During their research, grave misunderstandings arose between Rosalind Franklin and Maurice Wilkins, a fellow researcher who was second in command of the project. He assumed Franklin would work as his assistant and present evidence for his team to analyze. Franklin, on the other hand, assumed she was to work on the DNA project alone. Eventually, this conflict of personalities deteriorated to the point that they would not speak to each other.

The unfortunate situation did not deter Franklin. Even though she worked in isolation with only a graduate student for assistance, she made ever-finer X-ray pictures of the DNA molecule and came very close to unlocking the secret of the DNA structure and how it reproduces itself. In 1952, she made a now-famous image that showed a distinctive X shape, a very good indication that DNA had a twisted, or helical, shape. But absolute proof of its structure, and because she could not yet provide it, she would not dare to make the crucial intuitive leap that would have suggested that DNA is a double helix, shaped like a twisted ladder.

Meanwhile, Watson and Crick at Cambridge University were also working on the structure of DNA without much luck. At one point, they had created a DNA model that was so wrong it embarrassed Sir Lawrence Bragg, the head of the department. As a result, he forbade them to do any more work on DNA.

In 1953, the American Nobel Prize-winning chemist Linus Pauling published a paper speculating that DNA had a helical structure. A serious race to discover DNA 's structure then began. Franklin and Watson argued over whether Pauling had enough evidence to prove his point. Wilkins, who sided with Watson, gave James Watson a copy of Franklin's famous DNA image without her knowledge. Then, with Pauling in the DNA race, Lawrence Bragg allowed Crick and Watson to resume their research. Soon another researcher at Kings College passed more of Franklin's data to the Cambridge researchers.

Having all the pieces they needed, Crick and Watson announced in March 1953 that they had solved the DNA puzzle. They created a model showing DNA as a twisted ladder with rungs made of four chemical bases. The same two bases always joined to make a rung. When it was time for DNA to reproduce itself, the ladder unzipped into halves, with each side having half a rung. Since the same bases that made up each rung always joined together, biochemicals could assemble on each half ladder to create two whole ladders identical to the original one. This same basic process allows the genetic code to be translated into RNA, a biochemical that copies DNA and acts as a blueprint for cells to create protein needed to carry out basic functions.

Putting the situation at Kings College behind her, Franklin took a position as head of a research group at Birkbeck College. There, she used her X-ray crystallography skills to study viruses made of RNA. She hoped to discover how these simple strands of protein and genetic material could reproduce and cause illness. Eventually, she collaborated with Watson and Crick on viruses and actually became good friends with Crick and his wife. But she never liked Watson, whom she called the "horrible American." At Crick's invitation, Franklin moved to the molecular biology laboratory at Cambridge. There she continued to study the structure of viruses, including the polio virus.

In her brief career, Rosalind Elsie Franklin contributed greatly to the new scientific field of molecular biology. She died of ovarian cancer on April 16, 1958. Since her death, scientists and other observers have speculated on whether Franklin should have been included in the Nobel Prize for the discovery of the DNA structure. Unfortunately, only living people are awarded Nobels, so no one will ever answer the question to satisfaction.

JANE GOODALL
1934-
Ethologist

Vanishing Animal

From the time Jane Goodall was a little girl, she loved animals and enjoyed observing them. Once she spent hours crouched in a hot chicken coop waiting to see how a hen laid an egg. And for as long as she can remember, she dreamed of going to Africa to study animals there. Her childhood dream came true. Not only did she go to Africa, but she also became the first person to make close observations of chimpanzees in the wild. Her findings and the fascinating books she wrote about them have made her one of the most famous naturalists in the world.

Jane Goodall was born on April 3, 1934, in London, England. Her father was an engineer and auto racer; her mother, a novelist. When World War II (1939-1945) broke out, Jane's father joined the army. Her mother took Jane and her sister Judy to Bournemouth on the south coast of England, where the girls could attend school. Although Jane loved to read, especially books about Africa and animals, she did not particularly like learning in a structured class environment. She much preferred to be outdoors playing with her dog or riding horseback. From the very beginning, she had a special feeling for animals.

After graduating from the equivalent of high school at age eighteen, Goodall worked as a secretary at Oxford University and as an assistant film editor in London. Then came her big chance to go to Africa. A friend's parents had bought a farm in Kenya and invited her to visit. Realizing that this was the chance of a lifetime, Goodall returned home to Bournemouth long enough to earn enough money to purchase a steamship ticket to Africa. After visiting her friend's family, Goodall took a job in Nairobi where she met the famous anthropologist Louis Leakey. As a result of this meting, Goodall began a new career and fulfilled her dream of studying animals in Africa.

Leakey hired Goodall as a secretary and asked her to accompany him and his wife, Mary, to a dig for prehistoric human fossils in Kenya's Olduvai Gorge. Earlier, the Leakeys had found important fossils of prehuman ancestors. To further their study of ancient hominids, Leakey considered monitoring the behavior of chimpanzees, the animals most closely related to modern humans. He would focus on the protected communities of chimpanzees on the Gombe Stream Game Reserve (now called Gombe National Park) on Lake Tanganyika.

Working with Goodall for some time convinced Leakey that she was the right person to carry out close observations of the chimpanzees. The fact that she did not have a college degree did not matter to him. In fact, for his purposes, he thought it was a plus. She would have no preconceived ideas about how to do things. She could develop her own observation techniques.

In 1960, Leakey obtained funds for the project and sent Goodall into the bush to set up her tent camp to observe chimps. She took with her some scouts, a cook — and her mother, because the authorities would not allow a woman to live alone in the wilderness. However, her mother stayed only a few months.

Because chimps in the wild are shy of humans, Goodall could not get very close to them for more than a year. Every day, she went into the forest with her binoculars and a notebook to look for chimps. In time, some of the animals got used to seeing her, and her regular routine became familiar to them. One day, a male chimp that Goodall called David Greybeard, appeared in camp and began eating the bananas that were hanging outside her tent. Realizing this was the breakthrough she had been waiting for, Goodall began leaving bananas wherever chimps could find them. This practice gradually won the chimps' trust and enabled her to make detailed observations of their behavior.

Goodall named all the chimps she observed. Over the years, she observed generations of chimps, including Flo, one of her favorites, and Flo's grandchildren and their offspring. During Goodall's observations, she learned some surprising things. Two findings became very important to zoologists and ethologists who study animal behavior. The first discovery was that chimpanzees are not strict vegetarians. They will hunt and kill other animals, including baby baboons. This realization prompted Goodall to carefully guard her son when he was a baby.

Goodall's second major finding was that chimps can make and use tools. She came to this conclusion after observing David Greybeard using a blade of grass to fish termites out of a mound and eat them. Later, he even stripped a twig and used it to retrieve termites. Referring to this, Goodall wrote. "I was really thrilled. David had used objects as tools . . . . He had actually made a tool. Before this observation, scientists had thought that only humans could make tools."

Before long, visitors began arriving at her Gombe research station. One of them was a Dutch baron and photographer, Hugo van Lawick, who had come to take pictures for the National Geographic Society. In 1964, he and Jane were married, and in 1967 Jane had a son, nicknamed Grub. When Grub was seven years old, she and and van Lawick divorced. Goodall then married Derek Bryceson, director of Tanzania National Parks. He died in 1980.

A year after marrying van Lawick, Jane Goodall received her doctorate in ethology. Cambridge University awarded her a Ph.D. for her work with chimpanzees. Only seven people before her had been awarded a doctorate from Cambridge without a bachelor's degree. After receiving her doctorate, Goodall returned to Gombe to continue her observations. Over the years, many graduate students came to learn from her and study the chimps.

Through her research, Goodall has learned that chimps display warmth and affection. They hold hands, kiss, and groom one another. They have a social order in which there are dominant males and females. But they also have a darker side. The group Goodall studied during the 1970s split into two communities and went to "war." Eventually, one community wiped out the other.

Goodall loves to use anecdotes to describe chimp behavior. She has written many papers, articles, and books. Among her most famous popular works are *My Friends, the Wild Chimpanzees* (1967), *In the Shadow of Man* (1971), *The Chimpanzees of Gombe* (1986), *My Life With the Chimpanzees* (1988), and *Through a Window* (1990). Her starring role in a National Geographic television series has made her a worldwide hero.

Goodall believes that chimpanzees have become an endangered species because of human activity. "I anguish over the suffering endured by hundreds of chimpanzees at the hands of humans," she says. "They suffer in the wild as their habitats are destroyed and as mothers are shot and their infants seized." Knowing that many baby chimps were being sold as pets or as laboratory animals for medical research, Goodall established the Jane Goodall Institute for Wildlife Research, Education, and Conservation in 1975. Today, in addition to supporting research, the foundation works to improve the lives of chimps in captivity. It sponsors research projects for observing chimps in zoos and campaigns for the humane treatment of laboratory animals. Through fund-raising and educational programs, Goodall tries to involve everyone in these projects — from professional zoologists to schoolchildren. Her institute sponsors pro-

grams (preschool through college) in thirty countries and is currently spreading across North America.

Jane Goodall spends much of her time traveling around the world, lecturing and educating the public about the importance of chimpanzees. But whenever possible, she returns to the Gombe research station to be with the chimps. "Chimpanzees have given me so much," she writes. "The long hours spent with them in the forest have enriched my life beyond measure. What I have learned from them has shaped my understanding of human behavior, of our place in nature."

Harriet Ann Boyd Hawes

1871-1945
Archaeologist

In 1900, the sight of two young American women riding on mules through the rugged country of Crete, an island southeast of Greece, was highly unusual. One of the women was interested in plants. The other, Harriet Boyd Hawes, was looking for clues to buried cities of the Minoan civilization that flourished on Crete from 3,000 through 1100 B.C. In the late 1800s, archaeologists had come to believe that the ancient Greek legends had a basis in fact. A German archaeologist had excavated at the site of Troy on the north coast of Turkey, and an English archaeologist had just uncovered a great royal palace at Knossos, the main Minoan city on Crete. Excitement was running high about the possibility of locating other Minoan sites, and Hawes was determined to find one. She succeeded in her quest. Slight of build but strong of will, she became the first woman to direct an archaeological excavation and publish the findings. She was also the first archaeologist to uncover an Early Bronze Age Minoan town.

Harriet Ann Boyd was born in Boston, Massachusetts, on October 11, 1871. She was the youngest child and only daughter of Alexander and Harriet Fay Boyd. When she was a year old, Harriet's mother died, leaving her to be raised by her father and four brothers. Alexander, Jr., her second oldest brother, had a great deal of influence on her young mind, sharing his love of ancient history with her. She grew up knowing the famous legends of King Minos of Knossos, who kept a mythical beast that was half-bull and half-man in the mazelike labyrinth under his palace on the island of Crete. The stories that filled her imagination in childhood eventually absorbed her thinking as an adult and influenced her choice of careers.

No one was surprised then when Harriet Boyd went to Smith College in Northampton, Massachusetts, and pursued a classical education, which involved the study of ancient Greek and Roman history, civilization, and language. After graduating in 1892, Harriet taught classics, first as a private tutor, later at a girls' finishing school in Delaware. In 1896, she went to Athens, Greece, to attend the American School of Classical Studies and get a graduate degree that would allow her to teach classics in colleges.

As part of her studies, Boyd was interested in doing fieldwork and excavations. At that time, however, women were not allowed to participate in archaeological excavations sponsored by the school. So she would have to find a way to get out into the field on her own. Using her own money and some of the grant money she had received for her graduate studies, Boyd financed an exploratory trip to Crete. Jean Patton, a friend who was interested in studying plants on the island, accompanied her. They chose Crete on the advice of British archaeologist Arthur J. Evans, who had discovered the Palace of Minos. At his suggestion, Boyd focused her digging at a place called Kavousi, where she discovered several tombs dating from the Iron Age.

After returning to America, Boyd used her research to obtain a master's degree from Smith College in Northampton, Massachusetts, and began teaching there. In 1901, certain that more archaeological sites remained to be discovered at Kavousi, she obtained funding from the American Exploration Society of Philadelphia and returned to Crete. There, in a region of Kavousi called Gournia, she found an ancient town. Immediately, she organized a dig. But when classes were ready to begin at Smith College, she returned to Northampton and resumed teaching. In 1903 and 1904, she returned to Kavousi when college classes were not in session and directed the excavations.

As the first woman in charge of an excavation, Boyd had become internationally famous. Her discovery of a Bronze Age town populated by ordinary people provided a valuable contrast to the ancient lifestyles being uncovered in Minoan palaces. The event brought her public attention and sent her on a national lecture tour in 1902 to describe her findings.

While doing fieldwork at Kavousi, Harriet Boyd had met Charles Henry Hawes, a British anthropologist. They were married in 1906 and eventually had two children. With Charles, she wrote a popular book in 1901 called *Crete, the Forerunner of Greece*. Thereafter, her career path basically followed that of her husband's. When he went to the University of Wisconsin in 1908, she did also, and when he transferred to Dartmouth College in New Hampshire in 1910, the family followed. In 1919, Charles Hawes became assistant director and then associate director of the Boston Museum of Fine Arts. The family then settled permanently in Boston, and Harriet Hawes became a lecturer at Wellesley College in 1920 until her retirement in 1936.

In addition to her archaeological interests, Hawes had a social conscience and a strong sense of justice. Out of compassion, she had volunteered as a nurse during the Greco-Turkish War in 1897 and during the Spanish American War in 1898. During World War I (1914-1918), she went to Greece to establish a field hospital and then helped set up a volunteer unit of Smith College women to serve as relief workers in France. She also was sympathetic to the U.S. labor movement to the point of being sued for aiding workers on strike at a shoe factory in Cambridge, Massachusetts.

After retiring, Harriet and Charles Hawes moved to the Washington, D.C., area. Charles died in 1943. Harriet died two years later on March 31, 1945.

DOROTHY CROWFOOT HODGKIN

1910-1994
Physical Chemist, X-Ray Crystallographer

At the age of ten, Dorothy Crowfoot discovered the beautiful world of crystals. From a chemistry text for governesses, she learned how to grow brilliant blue crystals of copper sulfate. Oddly enough, in England at that time, simple chemistry was considered a suitable hobby for refined ladies. But the study of crystals became much more than a hobby for Dorothy Crowfoot. It became her life's work. She developed great expertise in X-ray crystallography, a technique that uses X rays to probe the very atoms from which crystals are made. Using X-ray crystallography, she discovered the structure of vitamin B12, insulin, and penicillin. In 1964, she was awarded the Nobel Prize for Chemistry for this work.

Dorothy Crowfoot was born in Cairo, Egypt, on May 12, 1910. Her father was a British colonial administrator when Egypt was still a British colony. When Dorothy was four years old, World War I (1914-1918) broke out, and she and her sisters were sent to stay with relatives in England, out of harm's way. In high school, she began showing interest in chemistry, which she often studied on her own. In a laboratory set up in the attic of her home, she learned to use surveyors' chemicals to analyze minerals. There she also read about the X-ray and crystal experiments of Henry and Lawrence Bragg. Little did she know that these early experiences would become a vital part of her life.

In 1927, Crowfoot became one of the few women to attend Oxford University. By her second year, she was probing the interior of crystal molecules with X rays. After graduating in 1932, she went to study crystallography at Cambridge, where the Braggs and other X-ray crystallographers were working with crystals of ever greater complexity, including proteins. The Braggs believed in equal employment opportunities for women. As a result, the field of X-ray crystallography acquired a large number of women experts.

In 1934, Somerville College at Oxford University offered her a teaching position and a chance to work on her doctorate. With some reluctance, she left the comfortable, social atmosphere of Cambridge and returned to Oxford, despite the fact that women were barred from the faculty chemistry club there.

Amid all this change, she learned that she had rheumatoid arthritis, a painful disease that cripples hands and feet. Determined not to let this disease control her life, she threw herself into her work, enduring the painful condition in silence. Her Oxford lab in the basement of a museum that housed dinosaur bones and archaeological artifacts resembled the dungeon of a haunted castle. There, she and her students set up microscopes and X-ray equipment and began expanding the limits of what the new technique of probing atoms with X rays could do. By analyzing the spots on X-ray film and applying complex mathematical calculations, she deciphered the arrangement of carbon, hydrogen, and oxygen atoms in the cholesterol molecule.

Although she was totally involved in her work, she still had time for a personal life and marriage. In 1937, she married Thomas Hodgkin, who shared her concern for the poor of the world and her political and philosophical beliefs. Eventually, they had three children — two girls and a boy.

By 1940, Hodgkin was working on penicillin, a newly discovered antibiotic produced by a natural mold. By then, Great Britain was embroiled in World War II (1939-1945), and penicillin's potential for treating infected wounds made it a high priority. To handle the astronomical number of calculations involved in deciphering the X-ray data, Hodgkin used one of the earliest IBM analog computers. By 1946, she was able to make a 3-D model of the penicillin molecule, which pharmaceutical companies later used to develop synthetic versions of the drug.

During this time, she was given a more prestigious appointment to Oxford University and a large laboratory, where she undertook the study of vitamin B12, a large complex molecule. She obtained her first X-ray picture of B12 in 1948, but it was not until 1956 that she completed the analysis of its 3-D structure. Hodgkin then turned her attention to the structure of insulin, which her team clarified in 1969.

For her scientific achievements, Dorothy Crowfoot Hodgkin received many honors in addition to the Nobel Prize, including Britain's Order of Merit and the Royal Medal of the Royal Society. As her scientific reputation grew, so did her reputation as an extraordinarily gentle person. The Nobel Prize-winning molecular biologist Max F. Perutz called her "the gentle genius." In 1977, she retired to a small house north of Oxford. Her husband died in 1982. Although she was crippled by arthritis and wheelchair-bound, she continued to travel worldwide to attend scientific meetings and peace conferences until her death on July 19, 1994.

Helen (Battles) Sawyer Hogg

1905-
Astronomer

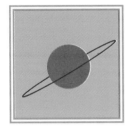

The train ground to a stop in the middle of a barren field and a troop of young college women descended into freezing air and knee-deep snow. The sky, which had been clear and bright, began to darken, and the countryside was bathed in an eerie light. Along with sister students from Mt. Holyoke College, Helen Sawyer witnessed the spectacle of the 1925 total eclipse of the sun. Anne Sewell Young, the inspiring astronomer, teacher, and director of Mt. Holyoke's observatory, had arranged for a specially chartered train to take the entire student body some 100 miles from the campus in South Hadley, Massachusetts, to central Connecticut where the view of the eclipse would be perfect. It was a day that Helen Sawyer never forgot. The experience convinced her to pursue a career in astronomy that ultimately has contributed to our understanding of the Milky Way Galaxy.

Helen Sawyer was born on August 1, 1905, in Lowell, Massachusetts. After the marriage of her older sister when Helen was five or six years old, Helen became, in essence, an only child. Her father, a banker, took her on nature walks along the Merrimac River. Her mother, a former teacher, introduced her to the wonders of rocks, flowers, and the constellations in the night sky. Helen was also influenced by Leonora Battles, a distant relative who lived with the Sawyers and who was one of the best elementary school teachers in Lowell.

When Helen enrolled at Mount Holyoke College, she had no intention of becoming an astronomer. Chemistry was her main interest. But after taking an astronomy course with Anne Sewell Young, she changed her major to astronomy and focused her attention on the groupings of stars called globular clusters, just outside the Milky Way Galaxy. A number of circumstances then came together to set the course of her future career. Annie Jump Cannon, the famous astronomer at Harvard College Observatory who had cataloged more than 300,000 stars, visited Mount Holyoke and was introduced to Helen Sawyer. Because the director of the Harvard Observatory, Harlow Shapley, was also interested in globular clusters, Helen Sawyer became the object of their attention. Believing that Helen could be helpful to Shapley, Ms. Cannon arranged a scholarship for Helen to Radcliffe College and the Harvard Observatory. There, she became an assistant to Shapley and began the work that would lead eventually to a Ph.D. in astronomy in 1931.

In the early 1900s, astronomers generally believed that the sun was the center of the Milky Way. But in 1917, Shapley began questioning that belief. He noted that the globular clusters were many thousands of light-years away from Earth and appeared to be orbiting a point he thought was the center of the Galaxy. By studying the light the clusters give off, he calculated that our solar system is about 50,000 light-years away from the galactic center. Later,

astronomers discovered that the space between the stars is filled with gas and dust that partially absorbs starlight, and when this is taken into account, calculations indicate that the solar system is more like 30,000 light-years from the center of the Galaxy.

The importance of using globular clusters to estimate distance became even more important when astronomers discovered variable stars within these clusters. Variable stars grow brighter and dimmer at regular intervals. Astronomer Henrietta Swan Leavitt discovered a formula for calculating the distance to a variable star based on the time of the interval between the brightest and the dimmest phase of the star. In the discovery and cataloging of these variable stars in globular clusters, Helen Sawyer made major contributions to astronomy.

While she was working on her doctorate, Sawyer met a Canadian astronomy student named Frank S. Hogg. In 1929, he was awarded the first Ph.D. in astronomy from Harvard. A year later, he and Helen were married. In 1931, Frank joined the staff of the Dominion Astrophysical Observatory in Victoria, British Columbia. Although there was no appointment for Helen, she was allowed to use the observatory's 72-inch reflecting telescope to take photographs of globular clusters. During this time, the first of their three children was born. On the nights that Helen ascended to the telescope platform at the top of the dome to take her pictures, she and Frank brought their infant daughter bundled up with blankets in a clothesbasket. He watched the baby and operated the mechanisms that controlled the telescope and the dome.

In 1936, the Hoggs moved to the David Dunlap Observatory at the University of Toronto where both enjoyed successful careers. Frank became the head of the observatory. Helen became a research assistant — her first paid job as an astronomer. She completed a major survey of variable stars and published her first catalog in 1939. Later, she worked at the University of Arizona, where she photographed the southern sky. Eventually, Helen discovered many new variable stars and published a second catalog in 1955. After Frank died in 1951, Helen took over many of his professional responsibilities. In addition to her research, she produced an astronomy column for a Toronto newspaper and contributed to several popular science encyclopedias. Much later, in 1976, she wrote a book called *The Stars Belong to Everyone*. That same year Helen Hoggs retired as an active professor of astronomy and became professor emeritus.

GRACE MURRAY HOPPER

1906-1992
Computer-Scientist, Navy Admiral

 Nothing does more to disprove the myth that girls and women do poorly in math and computer science than the life and work of Rear Admiral Grace Murray Hopper. She helped develop the basic technology that made modern computing possible. She was on the scene when the first enormous mechanical and vacuum tube computers were made, and she helped unravel the chaos created by early electronic computer programs that were totally incompatible with one another. Not only did this small and wiry woman make important contributions to developing computer programming language, such as COBOL, but she also helped coin the term "bug" that computer buffs know so well. "Amazing Grace" is what her admirers called her, a nickname earned by daring to envision a future that few people in the early days of computing could — and then taking risks to make it happen. "A ship in port," she loved to say, "is safe. But that is not what ships are built for."

Grace Murray was born on December 9, 1906, in New York City, the eldest of three children. Her parents, unlike most at that time, believed that girls should have the same opportunities as boys. Her father, an insurance broker, never reprimanded young Grace when she took apart the family's clocks to see how they worked. In fact, he even bought her a clock of her own to experiment with. Encouraged to attend college, she graduated from Vassar College in 1928 and went on to earn a Ph.D. in mathematics from Yale University in 1934. While in graduate school, she married Vincent Foster Hopper. They divorced in 1945.

During World War II (1939-1945), Grace Hopper became acquainted with the two great loves of her life — the Navy and computers. In December of 1943, she fulfilled what she saw as her patriotic duty by joining the U.S. Navy. She was commissioned as a lieutenant junior grade in the WAVES, the women's branch of the Naval Reserve. Her orders were to go to Harvard University in Cambridge, Massachusetts, and report to the Bureau of Ordnance Computation Project.

When Hopper walked into the basement laboratory at Harvard University, she saw a huge computing machine, 51 feet long and 8 feet high. It was the Mark I — the first big digital computer. Even though it weighed more than 5 tons and contained 500 miles of wire, it did not have anything like the computing power of a 1990s home computer. Instead of a keyboard and mouse, punch cards and paper tape were used to enter data into the Mark I. Instead of electronic circuits etched on silicon chips, mechanical relay switches controlled the computer's operations. And before the Mark I could do anything, operators had to program it. Hopper's assignment was to program Mark I to calculate how large an area could be cleared by a minesweeping device.

For the remainder of the war, Hopper worked in computer operations. When the war was over, she remained in the Naval Reserve and continued to work on computers at Harvard. She and her colleagues built a more advanced computer, the Mark II. One summer day, while working on it, the computer stopped. Upon opening the computer case, they found a moth jamming one of the relay switches. They plucked out the moth with tweezers, literally "debugging" the device. Thereafter, according to Hopper, the term "computer bug," entered everyday language.

In 1946, Hopper, who was still in the Naval Reserve, joined the Eckert-Mauchly Computer Corporation. They were the developers of ENIAC, which operated by means of 18,000 vacuum

tubes, and BINAC, which used magnetic tapes for storing data. Hopper's job was to teach employees of defense contractors to use BINAC in developing guided missiles. Programming these machines was very difficult and required highly trained mathematicians who could write commands in machine language consisting of long strings of 0s and 1s. These digits indicated whether a switch or a circuit should be open or closed.

In the early 1950s, Eckert-Mauchly, Remington Rand, and the Sperry Corporation all merged and built the famous UNIVAC, the first commercial computer. But in order for this and other commercial computers to win public acceptance, programming would have to be made easier. So Hopper and her colleagues accepted the challenge and developed subroutines that could be used over and over again for common functions. Then Hopper found a way for the computer to copy subroutines, thus inventing the compiler. She programmed the computer to, in effect, copy and paste subroutines into programs she was writing. Building on this programming technology, she invented a shorthand for writing programs. Later, she developed an English-language programming system that formed the basis for a data-processing language called FLOW-MATIC.

Because many programmers were developing different computer languages in the 1950s, Hopper feared that soon computers and computer experts would not be able to understand each other. So in 1959, computer experts formed a panel to develop a language for business use. Hopper, as technical adviser, had a great deal of influence on the outcome. The language that emerged — COBOL — became the standard for business and government.

After a brief retirement from the Navy in 1966, Hopper returned to active duty to solve problems that had arisen with various versions of COBOL. She came up with a standard not only for the Navy but for the entire U.S. government. She rose through the military ranks, becoming a rear admiral in 1985, a rank she held when she retired permanently from the Navy in 1986 at the age of seventy-nine. Despite her retirement, she continued to lecture and to learn all she could about developments in computer technology. "The day I stop learning is the day I die," she said. She stopped learning on January 1, 1992, at her home in Arlington, Virginia.

Ida Henrietta Hyde

1857-1945
Physiologist

The Midwest had been in the grip of a long drought in 1871, when on a fateful October night, a fire broke out on the South Side of Chicago. The city, built mainly of wood, was like a tinderbox. The flames of the Great Chicago Fire swept northward and eastward, destroying property worth about $200 million, including the business of Ida Hyde's mother. In the wake of the devastation, Ida had to leave school and go to work. Her enduring desire to learn, however, brought her back to college at the age of twenty-four. From then on, Hyde compiled an impressive list of "firsts" for women: the first to receive a degree from the University of Heidelberg in Germany, the first to conduct research in the laboratories of Harvard Medical School in Massachusetts, and the first woman member of the American Physiological Society. These "firsts" were not only testimony to her brilliance as a scientist, but also to her ability to overcome the widespread prejudice in the 1800s against women who wanted to be scientists.

Ida Henrietta Hyde was born on September 8, 1857, in Davenport, Iowa. She had two sisters and a brother. Her parents had come to the United States from Germany and had shortened their name from Heidenheimer to Hyde. Eventually, the family moved to the rapidly growing city of Chicago, where things apparently went well until the Great Chicago Fire.

At the age of sixteen, Ida Hyde was apprenticed to a women's hat company, where she worked for seven years. During that time, she attended a school for working people called the Chicago Athenaeum. She managed to spend one year at the University of Illinois when she was twenty-four years old, but then ran out of funds. After working seven more years as a teacher in the Chicago public schools, Hyde at last was able to continue her education, this time at Cornell University in Ithaca, New York. After graduating in 1891, she pursued studies in physiology and zoology at Bryn Mawr College, a newly founded women's school in Pennsylvania.

It was apparent from the start that Hyde was no ordinary student. Her work was noticed by a zoology professor from the University of Strasbourg in Germany, who invited her to study with him. With the help of a fellowship from a women's academic organization, Hyde went to Germany to work on her doctorate. There, a wall of discrimination confronted her.

First, the University of Strasbourg would not allow her to take the entrance examination for the Ph.D. program because she was a woman. Refusing to be discouraged, Hyde next applied at the University of Heidelberg. With the help of the German Ministry of Education and a German Grand Duke, the faculty was finally persuaded to accept Hyde as a doctoral candidate. After being accepted, however, Hyde faced another hurdle — resistance from the professor with whom she wished to work. He did not believe there was any useful role for a woman in science.

Keeping her sense of humor, Hyde wrote an amusing account of her trials entitled "Before Women Were Human Beings." Somehow she prevailed against all the negative forces at the university and was awarded a Ph.D. in physiology in 1896. She was almost forty years old before she was able to begin her research and teaching career.

Hyde carried out her research at the Zoological Station in Naples, Italy; Harvard Medical School in Boston, Massachusetts; Woods Hole Oceanographic Institution on Cape Cod, Massachusetts; and the University of Kansas in Lawrence, where she moved in 1898 to become an assistant professor of zoology. After the university established a physiology department, she became a full professor and department head. She was also a professor at the school of medicine. Always eager to add to her own knowledge, Hyde attended summer sessions at Rush Medical College in Chicago from 1908 through 1912.

Throughout her lifetime, Hyde made major contributions to the understanding of the nervous and respiratory systems and how they evolve in embryos. During the early 1900s, physiologists were studying how muscle, nerve, and organ tissue functioned. They knew that individual cells sent and received electrochemical signals that cause such reactions as muscle contractions. In 1921, Hyde was the first scientist to develop a tool for delivering or removing fluid from an individual cell, while at the same time stimulating the cell electrically. This tool, called a microelectrode, is essential to the study of neurobiology. Because Hyde's invention did not become widely known, the microelectrode was reinvented in the 1940s.

Although Hyde won recognition and honors for her professional accomplishments later in life, she could never forget the discrimination she experienced as a young woman. As a result, she was active in the women's suffrage movement, in efforts to establish high academic standards for women, and in helping women scholars financially. She gave $25,000 to establish an American Association of University Women fellowship.

After retiring from the University of Kansas in 1921, Ida Henrietta Hyde spent a year at the University of Heidelberg doing research on the effects of the radioactive element radium on living organisms. She then moved to California and lived in Berkeley until her death on August 22, 1945.

Mae C. Jemison

1956-
Astronaut, Physician, Biomedical Engineer

Each time mission control went through the final countdown and the TV screen showed a big Saturn rocket roaring off the launch pad with an *Apollo* spacecraft and its astronauts, Mae Jemison knew she was watching more than television. She was watching her destiny. She was certain that one day she would be an astronaut and the spacecraft seen on the TV screen would be carrying her. But the road to that destiny led her to many other places first — to medical school in New York City; to a refugee camp in Thailand; to a commitment with the Peace Corps in West Africa; to medical practice in Los Angeles, California; and finally, to the U.S. astronaut training facility in Houston, Texas. There, on September 12, 1992, TV screens across America showed the liftoff of the space shuttle *Endeavour* carrying Mae Jemison, the first African-American woman to fly in space.

Mae C. Jemison was born in Decatur, Alabama, on October 17, 1956, to Charlie Jemison, a maintenance supervisor, and Dorothy Jemison, a schoolteacher. When Mae was three years old, her family moved to the south side of Chicago, where she, her brother Charles, and her sister Ada grew up.

Jemison's parents always stressed the importance of getting a good education. And the Jemison children followed their advice. Mae's sister eventually became a psychiatrist, and her brother became a real estate broker.

Young Mae was curious about all sorts of things and spent long hours in the library. She was very interested in science, especially in the study of anthropology, archaeology, animal extinctions, and astronomy. At Morgan Park High School, she became fascinated with biomedical engineering.

She was consistently on the honor roll and won a National Achievement Scholarship to Stanford University in California. There she earned two bachelor's degrees, one in chemical engineering and another in African and Afro-American studies. But Jemison was also interested in dance and theater productions. "Science is very important to me," she once told a biographer, "but I also like to stress that you have to be well-rounded. One's love for science doesn't get rid of all the other areas."

After graduating from Stanford in 1977, Jemison immediately enrolled at Cornell University Medical College in New York City, earning her M.D. degree in 1981. While in medical school, she spent one summer working as a volunteer at a Cambodian refugee camp in Thailand. Following graduation, and completing graduate training, she became the Area Peace Corp Medical Officer in West Africa. She returned to the United States in 1985 and began practicing as a physician with a Health Maintenance Organization in Los Angeles. Although this was interesting work and she loved helping people, Jemison was still determined to become an astronaut.

Intending to become a candidate, Jemison applied to the National Astronautics and Space Administration. In the meantime, her continued love for biomedical engineering led her to take additional classes at the university. When the space shuttle *Challenger* exploded in space in January 1986, killing all the astronauts on board, the entire U.S. space program was put on hold. Mae Jemison's long-range plans were temporarily on hold, too. Although the *Challenger* disaster pointed out the risks and dangers of space flight, Jemison wasn't deterred. After reapplying, she was accepted in 1987.

In 1988, Jemison finished her astronaut training and qualified as a mission specialist, a scientist responsible for technical operations and experiments. Her ground duties included helping to check out shuttle payloads, computer software, and the thermal tiles that protect the orbiter from burning up during reentry into Earth's atmosphere. Not until September 12, 1992, did her dream of actually flying in space come true. Jemison's first flight in space was aboard the *Endeavour*, which carried a laboratory called Spacelab-J, developed by Japan. This marked the first joint space mission undertaken by Japan and the United States. Jemison and the other six crew members aboard the *Endeavour* tested the effects of weightlessness on animals such as flies, hornets, fish, frogs, and humans.

Mae Jemison's flight into space was truly international and in keeping with her viewpoint of space travel. "Space exploration," she told a newspaper reporter just before her historic flight, "is a birthright of everyone who is on this planet . . . . it is something that eventually we in the world community are going to have to share." Her historic flight is memorialized in a mural called "Black Americans in Flight" at the Lambert-St. Louis International Airport in St. Louis, Missouri. In 1993, she was inducted into the National Women's Hall of Fame in Seneca Falls, New York.

A Legacy of
Women Doctors

The appearance of women doctors on the medical scene today might seem like a relatively new development. But many scholars believe that the tradition of women as healers dates back to prehistoric times, when women were the likely ones to tend the sick and injured in their households. These women learned about plants with medicinal properties and perhaps how to do simple surgical procedures such as lancing boils, setting broken bones, and closing wounds. They were certainly the ones who helped with the birthing of children.

Archaeological records show that women physicians were prominent at the dawn of history. In ancient Egypt, for example, the goddess Isis was revered as the greatest of physicians, and her women followers attended ancient Egyptian medical schools. There was even a school of gynecology operated by and for women at the Temple of Såis in Lower Egypt.

As history progressed, women physicians became more rare. While the ancient Greeks worshipped the mythical Hygeia as the goddess of health, they discouraged real women from practicing medicine. Still, the names of a few extraordinary women physicians shine through the mists of time. Aspasia, a Greek physician in the first century A.D., gained fame for her work in obstetrics.

With the advent of Christianity, some women became deeply involved in the charitable work of caring for the sick. One of these was Fabiola, an upper-class Roman woman who converted to Christianity in the A.D. 300s and founded a hospital for indigent people suffering from "loathsome diseases."

There is evidence that women in in the Middle Ages in Europe were involved in practicing medicine. Not only were they midwives who delivered children and herbalists who dispensed medicines, but women were also students and faculty members at the medical schools of the universities of Salerno and Bologna in Italy. The outstanding woman physician of the Middle Ages was Trotula, who practiced and wrote about gynecology and taught at the medical school at Salerno in the 1000s.

With the rise of scientific medicine after the Renaissance, the names of women largely disappear from the historical records. Men were credited with the major advances in anatomy and physiology. And male physicians or barber-surgeons administered the common treatments for almost any illness — blood-letting and purging with powerful laxatives.

For most of the 1700s and 1800s, the medical schools in Europe were closed to women. Popular wisdom held that not only were women inferior intellectually, but a woman's "delicate nature" could not endure the sights, sounds, and smells encountered by practicing physicians.

In colonial North America, there were no medical schools at all until the late 1700s. To obtain medical training, a young man apprenticed himself to a practicing physician. When medical schools were finally established in the United States and Canada, none at first admitted women.

The first woman to receive a medical degree in the United States was Elizabeth Blackwell, who was born in England in 1821 and emigrated to New York City when she was eleven years old. When she decided to become a doctor, twenty-nine medical schools turned down her application simply because she was a woman. Almost as a prank, the students of Geneva Medical College in New York voted to accept her as a student, and she graduated in 1849. She and her sister Emily, who also became a doctor, opened a hospital in 1857 — the New York Infirmary for Women and Children — which mainly served the poor. Later, the Blackwell sisters added a medical school for women.

In the mid-1800s, a number of medical schools exclusively for women were established, and this was a direct outgrowth of the newly formed women's rights movement. Feminists such as Elizabeth Cady Stanton and Susan B. Anthony demanded that there be more women doctors. They won support for this idea from liberal Quakers in Pennsylvania, who in 1850 helped establish the first all-female medical school, the Women's Medical College of Pennsylvania (now the Medical College of Pennsylvania).

By the end of the 1800s, many state and private medical schools in the United States, Canada, and Europe had opened their doors to women. And many of the women graduates in the early and mid-1900s made great contributions to medical science. Some women doctors only treated patients and some — such as Italian neuroscientist Rita Levi-Montalcini and American biochemist Gerty Cori — only did research. Still others practiced a combination of both. One of these was the American pediatrician Helen Brooke Taussig (1898-1986), whose specialty was children's heart diseases. She discovered abnormalities in the hearts of blue babies, so called because their skin has a bluish tinge. The abnormality involved a blocked pulmonary artery that prevented the blood from picking up sufficient oxygen from the lungs to carry throughout the infant's body. With surgeon Alfred Blalock, Taussig created an operation for bypassing the blockage, thus allowing normal oxygen flow.

Some women doctors became involved with social reforms. Dr. Alice Hamilton (1869-1970), was one of the founders of industrial medicine. After graduating from the medical department of the University of Michigan in 1893, she moved to Chicago to work with her friend Jane Addams at the famous Hull House. She also served as an investigator for the United States Department of Labor, inspecting mines and factories for lead and other dangerous substances that could poison workers. Her efforts led to the establishment of workers' compensation laws. In 1919, Dr. Hamilton became assistant professor of industrial diseases at Harvard Medical School.

As more medical schools opened admissions to women, the all-female medical schools disappeared. And then it again became difficult for women to get into medical school. For most of the twentieth century, women accounted for about five percent of all U.S. doctors. After World War II (1939-1945), the situation grew worse. Women who applied to medical schools were often harassed and accused of trying to steal seats in medical schools from men.

Some observers believe that the lack of women doctors and medical researchers has been reflected in a lack of information about the health problems that afflict women today. Most major medical studies, such as those on the prevention and treatment of heart disease, have been conducted by men on men. Therefore, no one learned much about heart disease in women. And little attention was paid to debilitating diseases such as arthritis and osteoporosis, which afflict mainly older women.

But this situation began to change as more women, helped and encouraged by the second women's movement that began in the 1970s, entered the medical profession and took on major leadership roles in government and universities. The focus of federally funded research was turned toward women's health issues by cardiologist Bernadine Healy, who in 1991 became the first woman director of the National Institute of Health, a post she held until 1993. During that time, Healy set up the Women's Health Initiative, a long-range study involving many research institutions with the goal of obtaining vital information on the prevention and treatment of a host of illnesses that affect women.

The result of medical education opportunities opening up to women certainly benefits individuals who want to pursue medicine as a career. But it also promises to benefit the female half of the population as women doctors and medical researchers focus on the unique and specific health needs of women.

Irene Joliot-Curie

1897-1956
Nuclear Scientist

From the time she was a young girl, Irene Joliot-Curie's reasoning powers were apparent to the adults around her. Irene, like many children, was fascinated by dinosaurs. She knew that they lived long ago. Her grandfather, whom she regarded as old, also lived long ago. Therefore, she concluded, her grandfather must have seen dinosaurs.

This was one of the first times, but not the last, that her reasoning would lead her to the wrong conclusion. As an adult scientist, she almost made several momentous discoveries, but guessed wrong. She produced the subatomic particle called the neutron experimentally but did not identify it. She and her husband observed particles of antimatter, but failed to recognize them as such. Irene even came within a hair's breadth of discovering that atoms could be split, but the official discovery was made instead by Austrian physicist Lise Meitner and her colleagues. Despite these near-misses, Irene Joliot-Curie and her husband Frederick came up with the right conclusion that gave them their biggest scientific hit. They discovered artificial radioactivity, and for this they won the 1935 Nobel Prize for Chemistry.

Irene Curie was born in Paris on September 12, 1897, the first of two daughters born to Nobel Prize-winning scientists Marie and Pierre Curie. Her sister Eve was born in 1904. Two years later, tragedy struck the Curie household when Irene's father was killed by a horse-drawn wagon. After that, life for the Curies changed. Marie Curie took over her husband's position as professor of physics at the University of Paris while continuing to conduct her own research on radium and other radioactive elements. Irene and Eve, who had become children of a single working mother, were taken care of by grandparents and governesses.

Fame swirled around the Curie household, but the family was largely insulated from the publicity. In fact, the sisters regarded their mother as a sad, shy, timid person. Only when Irene accompanied her mother on official trips, as when Marie Curie received her second Nobel Prize in 1911, did Irene see the adoring crowds and appreciate that her mother was the most famous scientist in the world.

Over the years, Irene and her mother became very close. They wrote one another affectionate letters when Madame Curie was away on business or Irene was off at summer camp. Life with Irene was well documented by her artistic sister, who loved music and writing but cared nothing for science. Apparently, no two people could be more opposite than fun-loving, fashionable Eve and her somber sister Irene. In speaking of Irene, Eve once said, "All my efforts to get her to take care of her fine hair and to make up her face, with its firm and beautiful features . . . have been in vain." She said further, that "this young person, so unsociable, so slow-moving and hard to approach, lacked the dash of brilliant pupils. She had something better — knowledge once acquired was fixed firmly in her well-ordered mind."

Early on, Marie Curie recognized that her grave and quiet firstborn had a gift for scientific reasoning. And, unlike other young women of that day, Irene grew up understanding that her interest in science and math was perfectly normal. Marie took special interest in her

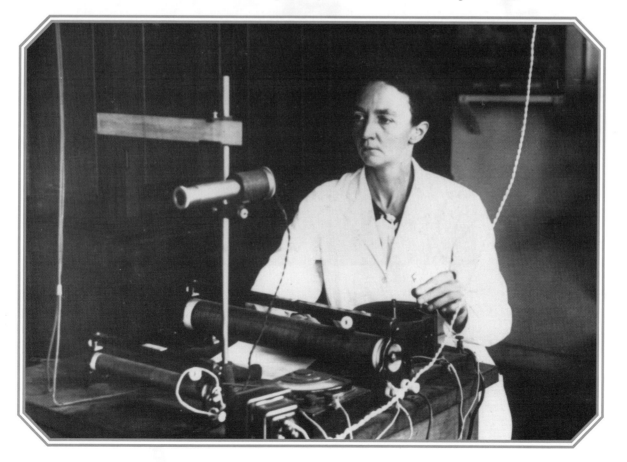

daughter's education. Madame Curie regarded the French schools as too rigid, relying on rote learning and drill rather than teaching people how to think. So she and other professors at the University of Paris organized an alternative school. Irene had some of the best minds in Paris for her instructors, including her mother, who taught her mathematics.

When Irene went off to the university, she had complete confidence in her academic abilities. Her sister Eve later wrote, "The examination periods for the bachelor's and master's degrees, which even made our mother in her time feverish and nervous, were for Irene Curie just like any other days. She went quietly to the Sorbonne [University of Paris], came back certain of being accepted, and then waited without emotion for the results, of which she was sure in advance." And when she went before a panel of professors to defend her dissertation, the last step toward earning a doctoral degree, there were one thousand people in the audience.

Marie Curie had as much confidence in Irene as Irene had in herself. When World War I broke out in 1914, Marie set aside her scientific research to organize mobile X-ray units for helping treat wounded soldiers at the battle front. She sent eighteen-year-old Irene off to the front lines by herself to help set up these X-ray units and train women to operate them.

Irene Curie began her scientific career as an assistant to her mother, who was at the time director of the Radium Institute of the University of Paris. Some of the workers there regarded Irene Curie as cold and aloof to the point of being unapproachable. But a young scientist, Frederick Joliot, saw much more in Irene, and they were married in 1926. Eventually they had two children, a boy and a girl.

The Joliot-Curies became serious research partners and worked together on projects involving radioactivity. Previously, nuclear scientists of Marie Curie's generation had established that the atom consists of a nucleus surrounded by negatively charged particles called electrons. They knew that radioactive atoms give off three types of rays — positive alpha rays, negative beta rays, and gamma rays, which are related to — but more powerful than — X rays. They also knew that by exposing uranium to radiation from these elements, they could change the atomic nucleus to create new elements. Finally, because of the discoveries of Marie and Pierre Curie, they knew of the highly radioactive elements polonium and radium.

Nuclear scientists of the Joliot-Curie's generation were in competition with one another to identify new elements. In the process, they made many unexpected findings. For example, they discovered the electrically neutral neutron and the fact that it, along with the positively charged proton, make up the nucleus of an atom. They also found that bombarding thin sheets of a metal with neutrons was an ideal way to probe atoms. The neutron would not be repelled by either the positive proton or the negative electron.

They had also begun to invent ingenious devices for detecting subatomic particles. One of these was the Geiger counter, which made a clicking sound each time it detected radioactive particles. Another was the cloud chamber, in which speeding subatomic particles left visible and distinctive vapor trails. The Joliot-Curies used both of these devices in their research.

While bombarding thin aluminum foil with alpha particles from polonium, Irene and Frederick made their greatest discovery. They observed neutrons and positrons (the antimat-

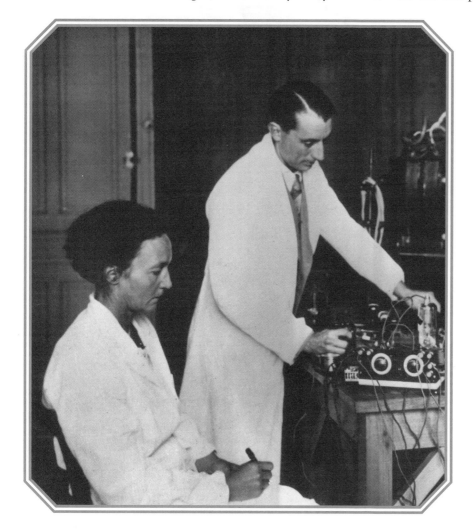

ter opposite of electrons) streaming out of the aluminum. When they took the polonium away and tested the aluminum with a Geiger counter, the unmistakable clicks told them it was radioactive. They analyzed what was happening and discovered that the nucleus had ejected a neutron and, in the process, had changed into an unusual type of radioactive phosphorus. The phosphorous nuclei soon underwent another change and became silicon. As a result of this experiment, the Joliot-Curies created the first artificially radioactive isotope, a form of an element that has the same number of protons but different numbers of neutrons. And for this they won a Nobel Prize. This work had significant and far-reaching applications, especially in medicine. Other isotopes were soon created, including a radioactive form of iodine, which was used to treat thyroid problems.

After discovering artificial radioactivity, the Joliot-Curies ceased working together on scientific problems. Frederick devoted his research to developing the atom smasher, or particle accelerator, while Irene directed the Radium Institute, a position she took over after her mother's death in 1934. She remained there until the German Army occupied France during World War II. Then, suffering from tuberculosis and concerned for her family's safety, she fled with her children to Switzerland. Frederick, who had joined the underground French Resistance and the Communist Party, remained behind to fight.

After the war, Frederick was considered a national hero. He became head of the French Atomic Energy Commission and Irene became a commissioner. Together, the Joliot-Curies virtually controlled France's nuclear program, which they maintained should focus only on peaceful uses. But anti-Communist sentiment was growing in the West, fueled by the Cold War with the Soviet Union. Under pressure from its allies, the French government fired Frederick because of his Communist Party ties, and in 1951, it did not renew Irene's term as a commissioner. Irene continued her work at the Radium Institute, but Frederick left research to work in international peace organizations.

By then, the years of radiation exposure were clearly taking a toll on the health of the Joliot-Curies. On March 17, 1956, at the age of fifty-eight, Irene died of leukemia, just as her mother had. Frederick died two years later of the same disease.

MARY NICOL LEAKEY

1913-
Anthropologist

The prehistoric past has always been part of Mary Leakey's everyday world. When she was just a little girl, she accompanied her father, a landscape painter, to southern France, where archaeologists had discovered caves filled with paintings of mammoths, bisons, and human hunters created by Stone Age artists as long as 30,000 years ago. As a schoolgirl, Mary had joined famous French archaeologists on expeditions into these underground art galleries and had helped uncover evidence of the Ice Age artists whose work covered the cave walls. She learned excavation techniques from these archaeologists and drawing techniques from her father. Later in life, these skills, along with her natural curiosity about the past, helped shed light on the mysteries about prehuman ancestors.

Mary Nicol was born on February 6, 1913, in London, England. Her father was a successful landscape painter, as was his father. On her mother's side, Mary's great-great-grandfather, John Frere, was the first to realize that there was a link between stone tools and early prehistoric people.

While Mary was growing up, she had no formal schooling because her father's painting career took the family away from home often. Instead, she learned from her father to read, draw, and love prehistory. He had an avid interest in ancient artifacts, especially Egyptian. In her autobiography, *Disclosing the Past* (1984), Mary credits her father, as well as her childhood experiences in the painted caves of France, with peaking her interest in the prehistoric world and a career in anthropology.

Mary was thirteen when her father died, and her mother thought it was time for her to get a formal education. Unfortunately, the halfhearted attempt to make Mary conform proved unsuccessful. She was used to being independent and learning from older, sophisticated people in an archaeological setting.

After Mary was expelled from two schools, her mother abandoned the idea and let fate take its course. As fate would have it, Mary met archaeologist Dorothy Liddell one summer at a late-Stone Age excavation site in England. This meeting made a deep impression on Mary who, like most women of the time, did not think the field of archaeology was open to women. She wrote in her autobiography, "Perhaps when I met Miss Liddell this first time, I absorbed there and then the notion that a career in archaeology was certainly open to women." With great interest, Mary Nicol pursued a career in archaeology, first serving as assistant to Dorothy Liddell on a late-Stone Age excavation in Devon, where she made drawings of stone tools, and later studying geology and archaeology at London University.

Her drawings caught the attention of another woman archaeologist, Gertrude Caton-Thompson, who was excavating in Egypt. Caton-Thompson asked Mary to make drawings of Egyptian stone tools. She also introduced her to Louis S. B. Leakey, a Cambridge University professor who was studying Stone Age cultures in Africa.

Louis Leakey, the son of missionary parents, had been born in Kenya and was familiar with Kikuyu language and culture. He asked Mary Nicol to provide drawings for a book he was writing. Their involvement quickly progressed from professional to personal. Divorcing his wife, Leakey married Mary in 1936. Thereafter, Africa became their home as well as the focus of their work at several excavation sites. In 1948, Mary made her first internationally famous find. On an island in Lake Victoria, she found the almost complete skull of an 18-million-year-old ape-like creature, later named *Proconsul*. But the excavations for which the Leakeys are best known were conducted in an area of Tanzania called Olduvai Gorge. There, beginning in the 1950s, Mary Leakey made some of the most spectacular finds of ancient prehuman fossils.

At the time the Leakeys began excavating at Olduvai, they had a family of three boys: Jonathon, born in 1941; Richard, 1944; and Philip, 1949. On fossil digs, the boys accompanied them along with a team of skilled African workers and several dogs that kept away wild animals and snakes. In 1959, Mary Leakey made a discovery at Olduvai that rocked the scientific world — the fossil remains of *Zinjanthropus* (later renamed *Australopithecus boisei*), a prehuman ancestor that lived about 1.75 million years ago. Often the boys helped dig up fossils. In fact, it was Jonathon who, in 1960, actually made the next big Leakey find. Louis named the remains Jonathon found *Homo habilis*, meaning "skillful man," one of the earliest creatures belonging to the same genus as human beings. Scientists believe this may have been the first creature to make stone tools. Other *Homo habilis* fossils, found by Richard Leakey in northern Kenya in 1972, were dated at 1.9 million years old.

The Leakeys became quite a team. Louis publicized the finds on lecture tours and fit them into the big picture of the evolution of humans in Africa. Mary did the painstaking work of uncovering, measuring, and cataloging the finds. Over time, however, the husband and wife team became estranged, disagreeing over scientific issues as well as family matters. In 1968, they agreed to separate.

When Louis died in 1972, Mary took over some of his public-speaking duties. She continued to do her own research and in 1978 led an expedition to Laetoli Tanzania on the Serengeti Plain near Olduvai Gorge, where the expedition found what Mary considered to be the most important find of all — a set of footprints made by humanlike creatures 3.7 million years ago. The footprints were perfectly preserved by ash from an ancient volcano. The fact that no tools were found in the fossil deposits around them supported a previous theory that humanlike creatures' ability to walk upright preceded their ability to make tools.

Among her many accomplishments was the study of Stone Age paintings in Tanzania. She published a book about them in 1983 — *Africa's Vanishing Art*. In the mid-1980s, she stopped directing the excavations at Olduvai and moved to a suburb of Nairobi, where she currently lives near her children and grandchildren.

Mary Leakey, a quiet, soft-spoken woman who could never settle down to a formal education, has received honorary doctorates from the world's most prestigious institutions, including Oxford and Yale universities. She has been given awards from geological societies and the Royal Swedish Academy. When asked by an interviewer what drove her to make such an impressive list of finds, Mary Leakey replied, "Curiosity. What made man *man?*"

Henrietta Swan Leavitt

1868-1921
Astronomer

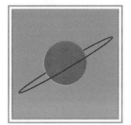

All her life, Henrietta Swan Leavitt was a deeply religious person. Her family's Puritan history stretched back to 1640, when her father's ancestors first landed in Massachusetts. Reflecting this Puritan heritage, she was quiet, conscientious, and totally devoted to her family, her church, and her work. Like another famous woman astronomer of her day, Annie Jump Cannon, Leavitt was almost totally deaf. And like Cannon, she went to work for Director Edward C. Pickering at the Harvard College Observatory. There Leavitt made a landmark discovery about stars called Cepheid variables that led to a way of determining the vast distances between the Milky Way and other galaxies.

Henrietta Swan Leavitt was born on July 4, 1868, in Lancaster, Massachusetts. She was one of seven children born to Henrietta and George R. Leavitt, a Congregational minister. As her father changed pastorates, the family moved to Cambridge, Massachusetts, then to Cleveland, Ohio.

Henrietta attended Oberlin College and in 1888 transferred to the Society for Collegiate Instruction of Women (now called Radcliffe College), where she began her study of astronomy. After graduating in 1892 and taking some time off to travel, she returned to Cambridge in 1895 to work as a volunteer at the Harvard Observatory. In 1902, she became a paid assistant, studying variable stars. She rapidly advanced, becoming head of the department of photographic photometry.

At that time, the advances and tools of physics and technology were being applied to the science of astronomy. Edward C. Pickering, the director of the observatory, had established an ambitious program to measure the brightness of stars using a technique called photometry. (A photometer is a device that translates light from a distant star into an electric current — the brighter the star, the stronger the current.)

Knowing that photographic plates are more sensitive than the naked eye to certain wavelengths of light, Pickering decided to establish a standard of brightness based on photographs of stars near the north celestial pole. Leavitt, who was then chief of the photographic photometry department, was assigned to carry out this survey of the sky. By 1917, using 299 photographic plates taken by thirteen telescopes, she determined a north polar sequence of stars ranging from a magnitude of 4 to 21. (Magnitude is the measurement of a star's brightness — the brighter the star, the lower its magnitude.) Until around 1940, astronomers used this north polar sequence of stars as standard reference points to calculate the precise positions of other stars in the Milky Way.

During the early 1900s, Leavitt also studied stars in a region of the sky called the Magellanic Clouds. We now know the Magellanic Clouds are nearby galaxies. But at that time, astronomers could not be certain that other galaxies existed outside the Milky Way because the telescopes were not yet powerful enough to produce clear images of these distant objects. The images they captured of heavenly bodies outside the Milky Way appeared only as bright clouds. However, after taking a sequence of photographs of these clouds, Leavitt identified stars whoses brightness varied over a period of time. By analyzing changes in the photographs and applying mathematical formulas, she discovered an important link between the star's time period and its absolute or true brightness. The longer the time period during which the star's brightness varied, the greater was the star's absolute brightness.

The difference between absolute and apparent brightness in a star is the same as in other glowing objects, such as a car's headlights. Up close, headlights are blinding. But off in the distance, they appear to be mere pinpoints of light. Knowing how bright a star or a headlight actually is and comparing it with how bright it appears to be can help us measure how far away it is. Leavitt's discovery of the link between time period and brightness in Cepheid variables gave astronomers an easy way to calculate the true brightness of this type of star. Her research led the way for another American astronomer, Harlow Shapley, to calculate the true brightness of other stars. Eventually, astronomers discovered that Cepheids appear in other galaxies, thus making them "standard candles" by which scientists could calculate the size of the Milky Way and the vast distances of intergalactic space.

Although Henrietta Swan Leavitt made major contributions to the field of astronomy, she did not receive major honors in her lifetime. She lived and worked quietly and died of cancer on Dececember 12, 1921.

RITA LEVI-MONTALCINI
1909-
Neuroscientist

The death of a beloved governess from stomach cancer marked a turning point in Rita Levi's life. She vowed to become a doctor. But this would not be easy given her family situation. The Levi family was headed by her hot-tempered father, Adam Levi, who ruled with an iron hand. As a young girl, Rita had watched her mother submit totally to his demands. Rita concluded that this was not the type of life she wanted to live. And through sheer perseverance, not only did she escape the fate of her submissive mother, but she also went on to become a scientist whose discoveries about the nervous system won her a Nobel Prize. She became a distinguished professor in the United States and the director of a major research laboratory in Rome, Italy.

Rita Levi was born in the Italian city of Turin on April 22, 1909, along with her twin sister, Paola. (Eventually, Rita included her mother's maiden name — Montalcini — in her name.) Rita's mother was a gifted painter, but she was overshadowed by her husband who dominated the entire family. Although Rita feared her father, she came to regard him as the most important figure in her life.

Adam Levi came from a large family of Jewish intellectuals, whose forebears had come to Italy from Israel in the days of the ancient Roman Empire. Most of Adams's sixteen brothers became lawyers. Of his two sisters, one earned a doctorate in mathematics; the other, in literature. Both sisters had unhappy marriages, which Adam attributed to their education. As a result, he would have none of it in his immediate family. Believing that women should be subordinate to men, he sent his daughters to finishing school to learn to be gracious wives and mothers.

In the shadow of this man, young Rita was shy, timid, and fearful. But, inside her, a powerful resentment was growing. Knowing she could not accept the kind of life her mother led, Rita decided that she would never marry or have children. She would, instead, become a doctor. Naturally, her father said it was out of the question. But with the help of her mother, Rita eventually persuaded him to allow her to try. After six months of being tutored in mathematics, science, Latin, and Greek, Rita absorbed the educational equivalent of what in the United States would be high school and two years of college. She passed the entrance exams — first in the rankings — and in 1931, at the age of twenty-one, became a student in the Turin School of Medicine.

In medical school, Levi-Montalcini attended strictly to her studies. Because she was one of only seven women among three hundred male medical students, she decided to dress in a very plain manner. By the end of her professional career, however, she was regarded as a most elegant and fashionable woman.

While in medical school, Levi-Montalcini met Professor Giuseppe Levi. Although not a relative, he would become like a second father to her — a teacher, a mentor, and a lifelong friend. Like her father, he was domineering and hot-tempered. He was also an expert on the microscopic study of cells. Under his guidance, Levi-Montalcini began to study nerve cells and structures. She learned how to stain nerve cells from chicken embryos so that they were visible in great detail.

In 1936, after graduating from medical school, Levi-Montalcini decided to specialize in neurology and obtained a post as Giuseppe Levi's assistant. But the rise of fascism in Italy and the outbreak of World War II (1939-1945) disrupted her career. Because the Italian dictator Benito Mussolini had issued a decree forbidding Jews to hold academic posts, both she and Levi lost their jobs. They found research positions in Belgium, but when the Germans also invaded Belgium, Levi-Montalcini returned to Turin. She tried to practice medicine among the poor, but fascist laws would not allow Jews to write prescriptions. So, upon a friend's advice, she set up a makeshift research lab in her bedroom.

After purchasing a microscope and fashioning tiny surgical instruments out of needles, Levi-Montalcini resumed her research on chicken embryos, which she obtained from fertilized eggs. Following the work of Viktor Hamburger at Washington University in the United States, she began experimenting on nerve cells from chicken embryos to determine what effect developing limbs had on the development of the nerves serving those limbs. Eventually, Giuseppe Levi joined her research efforts. But this, too, came to an end.

In 1942, when the Allied forces began bombing Turin, Levi-Montalcini and her family escaped to the countryside. Taking her tiny lab with her, she set it up in the country house in the corner of the living room. When Mussolini's government fell a year later and the German Army began transporting Jews to death camps, Levi-Montalcini and her family fled again. After an unsuccessful attempt to escape to Switzerland, they went into hiding in Florence, Italy, under assumed names. Until British troops arrived in 1944, Levi-Montalcini and her twin sister worked at forging false identity cards for Jewish friends.

At the end of World War II, Levi-Montalcini published the results of her research on chicken embryos. Viktor Hamburger, after reading her article, invited her to come to St. Louis, Missouri, to work with him for a few months. In 1946, she accepted his offer and stayed at Washington University for more than thirty years.

During this time she made a remarkable discovery. After having read the results of a graduate student's experiment hypothesizing that fast-growing tumor tissues could affect the growth of nerve cells in chicken embryos, Levi-Montalcini repeated the experiment. She found that the nerve fibers actually sought out and grew into and around the tumor as though they were seeking some highly attractive substance. From these results, she made an intuitive leap: The tumor, she reasoned, must be releasing some unknown growth factor.

To test this idea, she turned to a friend and to the new technique of tissue culture — growing living tissues in lab dishes. Her friend, Hertha Meyer, who had fled to Rio de Janiero, Brazil, to escape the Nazis during the war, had a tissue-culture lab with the type of equipment Levi-Montalcini needed. As soon as she got a research grant, she flew to Rio with two live mice hidden in her bag and arrived at Meyer's door.

In Meyer's laboratory, Levi-Montalcini placed chicken blood, a piece of mouse tumor, and some nerve tissue in a glass dish, then waited for it to incubate. Within hours, the nerve tissue had grown, surrounding the tumor tissue with a halo that sent out rays of nerve fibers. Levi-Montalcini couldn't resist finding out what was causing the tissue to grow. She returned to St. Louis, where she worked with biochemist Stanley Cohen, to isolate and identify what she called the nerve growth factor. Six years later, they were successful. For their discovery of the nerve growth factor, Cohen and Levi-Montalcini shared the 1986 Nobel Prize for Physiology or Medicine.

Since then, more growth factors have been discovered. Growth factors have proved to be an extremely important class of substances. They even play a role in the development of cancer when the control of the gene coding for a growth factor is somehow altered. The faulty production of growth factor can help set off uncontrolled cell growth.

Levi-Montalcini's collaboration with Cohen ended in 1959, when he moved to Vanderbilt University in Nashville, Tennessee. In 1961, she received a National Science Foundation grant to set up a small research lab in Rome and began spending six months of the year there, living in a quiet, book-lined apartment with her twin, Paola, a painter. The Italian government funded the laboratory, which grew into a major research facility — the Laboratory of Cell Biology. Levi-Montalcini was its director from 1969 to 1979, when by law she had to retire. In 1977, she became professor emeritus at Washington University, where she had been a full professor since 1958.

In addition to receiving the Nobel Prize, Levi-Montalcini won many awards and honors during her career, including the U.S. National Medal of Science and the Lasker Award for medical research. She was a member of the most prestigious scientific organizations in the United States and Italy, including the Pontifical Academy of Sciences.

After she retired as director of the Laboratory of Cell Biology in Rome, Levi-Montalcini continued to volunteer at the laboratory and for organizations involved with degenerative diseases of the nervous system. In her eighties, this short, slim, gray-haired woman heads for work every day in her fashionable suits and high heels. "The moment you stop working," she says, "you are dead."

Antonia C. Maury

1866 – 1952
Astronomer

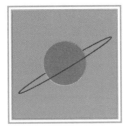

Antonia Maury's sparkling dark eyes reflected both her Portuguese ancestry on her mother's side and her free spirit. Her family's connections to the astronomical world of that day enabled her to find employment at the Harvard Observatory in Cambridge, Massachusetts, but her independent thinking brought her into direct conflict with the director of the observatory. Maury's work was not accepted at Harvard. It was a Danish astronomer who finally recognized the pioneering significance of her observations and conclusions, which were of major importance to the development of modern theoretical astrophysics.

Antonia Maury was born on March 21, 1866, in Cold Spring, New York. Her father, Mytton Maury, an Episcopalian priest, was an amateur naturalist and an acquaintance of astronomer Edward C. Pickering, director of the Harvard College Observatory. Her uncle, Henry Draper, was an amateur astronomer who made the first photographs of the sun's spectrum (rainbow colors of light) through a prism in a telescope. Antonia's aunt through marriage, Mary Anna Palmer Draper, endowed the Henry Draper Memorial at Harvard in 1886, allowing it to continue work on the spectra of stars in honor of her husband.

With a family like this, there was no question that Antonia would pursue higher education. She enrolled at Vassar College in Poughkeepsie, New York. There she studied philosophy, physics, and especially astronomy under Maria Mitchell, the first woman astronomer in America. Maury graduated with honors in 1887.

In 1888, she took a position at the Harvard Observatory, where astronomers were identifying and classifying various types of stars by analyzing the light coming from them. Maury was given the task of classifying the bright stars in the northern sky and was paid twenty-five cents an hour.

She worked with spectrograms taken with improved spectroscopes employing several prisms. These prisms better separated the bands or lines that reveal the pattern of light coming from the stars. Maury's job was to use these spectrograms to refine the classification system developed earlier by Edward C. Pickering and Williamina Fleming, Harvard's first woman astronomer. But the independent-minded Maury decided that this earlier classification system was inadequate.

Maury found that her spectrograms revealed hundreds of lines of varying widths and sharpness. She believed that these represented important dimensions in star classification. So she developed her own system. But Pickering thought this type of painstaking analysis was a waste of time. He did not believe that the level of detail Maury was uncovering had any significance for classifying stars.

Maury got no support from her aunt, who apparently did not like her. Mary Draper tried to influence Pickering against her niece while Antonia's father wrote letters to Pickering defending her. Worn down by this atmosphere, Antonio left Harvard in 1892 without finishing her research. However, Pickering and Maury finally reached an agreement, and she finished the work in 1896. It was published in 1897. Maury did not to return to Harvard for more than twenty years. She taught at Cornell and other schools while also lecturing. She was an avid ornithologist and conservationist, active in the movement to save the California redwoods.

The significance of Maury's work on stellar spectra was recognized by Danish astronomer Ejnar Hertzsprung, who had discovered that stars of the same color vary in size — some being dwarfs and others giants. Realizing that Maury's published catalog of the northern stars confirmed his findings, Hertzsprung urged Pickering to recognize her classification system. He said that not to do so would be like a zoologist detecting the difference between a whale and a fish but continuing to classify them together. Hertzsprung's discovery of Maury's work helped him create the Hertzsprung-Russell diagram, a tool for grouping stars according to their spectral class, size, and emission of radiant energy. With this groundwork, astronomers later developed theories about how stars are born, live out their lives, and die.

Maury returned to the Harvard Observatory in 1918. Two years later, Edward Pickering was succeeded by Harlow Shapely, who understood Maury's work and encouraged her research. She spent much of her time studying spectral binaries — double stars that can be detected only by the double spectral lines their light produces.

In 1943, the American Astronomical Society awarded Maury its Annie Jump Cannon Prize. Maury retired from Harvard in 1935, and for three years served as custodian of the Draper Park Observatory Museum at Hastings-on-Hudson, New York. She died on January 8, 1952.

Antonia C. Maury was a dreamer. She always regarded the vast expanses of the universe with awe. "But the human mind is greater yet," she said, "because it can comprehend it all." Antonia Maury's life is proof that she wanted to comprehend it all. Some astronomers believe that with the proper training and encouragement she could have been a great theoretician, advancing ideas about how stars form.

MARIA GOEPPERT MAYER

1906-1972
Theoretical Physicist

Maria Goeppert loved a good party. She enjoyed dancing and flirting with the young men invited to her mother's parties in Göttingen, Germany. Maria's father, who was a professor at the University of Göttingen, ranked high in the German social order. Frau Goeppert was one of the town's leading hostesses, and Maria, with her blue eyes and reddish-blonde hair, was known as "the beauty of Göttingen." But Maria Goeppert was more than just an attractive young woman. Her avid interest in nature and mathematics, combined with her obvious intelligence and ability, eventually led her to a science career and to the creation of a detailed model of the atomic nucleus, for which she won the Nobel Prize in Physics in 1963.

Maria Goeppert was born on June 28, 1906, in Upper Silesia, then part of Germany, but now part of Poland. She was the only child born to Maria and Friedrich Goeppert. Her father, in addition to being a professor of pediatrics at the University of Göttingen, was director of a children's hospital and founder of a day-care center for working mothers. Maria adored her father, who instilled in her a love of science. Together they searched for fossils and studied plants in the woods. He encouraged her to pursue a career in addition to marriage and motherhood, insisting that she acquire a good education so that she could support herself and develop her talents.

At this time, it was easy for boys to prepare for a university education at one of the boys' schools in Göttingen, but this was not the case for girls. Fortunately for Maria, a group of suffragettes had set up a small private school to prepare young women for university examinations, and she enrolled there at the age of fifteen. Three years later, however, Germany was plagued by runaway inflation, and the girls' school closed. Against the advice of their teachers, Maria and four other young women decided to take the university entrance examinations a year early. To the surprise of many, the women passed the exam and were enrolled at the university.

Maria studied mathematics and then physics at the University of Göttingen in the mid- to late-1920's, when the university was attracting some of the greatest mathematicians and physicists in the world. Maria came to know them all. Her mentor, Max Born, was one of the developers of quantum mechanics — a mathematical theory that predicts and describes the motions of subatomic particles just as classical Newtonian physics predicts and describes the motions of objects in the world of everyday experience. One aspect of quantum theory holds that radiant energy, such as light, travels in tiny packets called quanta. Maria's dissertation for her doctorate, which she received in 1930, involved aspects of light quanta, called photons.

In addition to great professors, the University of Göttingen attracted students who later became famous themselves. Many of these students became Maria's friends and admirers — chemist Linus Pauling, physicists Enrico Fermi, Eugene Paul Wigner, J. Robert Oppenheimer (who directed the effort to develop the atomic bomb), and Edward Teller (father of the hydrogen bomb). One of the young men who arrived in Göttingen in 1929 was a rich, handsome chemist from California, Joseph E. Mayer, who had come to the university to study quantum mechanics with physicist James Franck.

Looking for room and board, Mayer approached Frau Goeppert, who at that time was accepting student boarders. Like most of the young men who stayed with the Goepperts, Joe was attracted to Maria and soon came to respect her as one of the brightest women he had ever met. Maria returned Joe's love and affection and married him in 1930. They moved to the United States where they had two children, a girl born in 1933 — the year Maria became a U.S. citizen — and a boy in 1938.

Maria wanted it all — children, a dazzling social life, and a career as one of the world's top physicists. But for now, she had to settle for being a university professor's wife. Joe's first post was at Johns Hopkins University in Baltimore, Maryland. The university had no position for Maria because the rules did not allow the employment of married couples. The same was true when Joe went to Columbia University in New York City in 1939. However, Maria was able to volunteer her services as a physicist at Johns Hopkins and Columbia. She applied quantum theory to chemical problems involving crystals and dyes. With her husband, she wrote a mathematics book called *Statistical Mechanics*.

Joe and Maria were quite the dashing, daring couple. Like her mother, Maria loved to give wonderful parties. Both Joe and Maria were chain-smokers and heavy social drinkers. During Prohibition, they crushed enough grapes in a washing machine to make 100 bottles of wine. In the 1940s, when Maria was hospitalized for surgery, a colleague playfully smuggled her a bottle of Scotch. Although this type of high living was then regarded as fashionable and sophisticated, it may have taken a toll on Maria's health and robbed her of the opportunity to fully savor the triumphs of her career later in life.

When the U.S. government decided to build an atomic bomb during World War II (1939-1945), Maria was invited to work on the secret project. She collaborated with others to discover ways to enrich uranium for use in the bomb. But because Joe was away on weapons research, and Maria wanted to spend quality time with her children, she refused to work on weekends or when the children were sick. As a result, she was not given the most important projects. In fact, none of her work contributed to building the bomb. After the bomb was dropped on Japan in 1945, she was grateful that her efforts played no real role in its development. It was one less thing to feel guilty about.

In 1946, the University of Chicago invited both Mayers to join the faculty, even though only Joe was offered a salary. Maria's position remained unpaid, even after she was promoted to full professor. She did, however, earn a half-time salary as a senior physicist at the Argonne National Laboratory where she also worked.

In Chicago, Maria undertook the work that led to a Nobel Prize. It began with a project to determine the origin of the chemical elements. While cataloging the properties of the various elements, she noticed that some of them had stable nuclei. It was commonly known that atoms of many elements tend to decay into other elements when they lose some of the protons and neutrons of their nucleus. But Maria noticed that atoms with a certain number of protons or neutrons did not decay. These numbers were 2 (helium), 8 (oxygen), 20 (calcium), 50, 82, and 126. These numbers, which she found empirically in 1948, were dubbed "magic numbers."

In the 1930s, scientists pictured the nucleus as being like a drop of liquid with the protons and neutrons swimming around. In discovering nuclear fission, the Austrian physicist Lise Meitner envisioned this drop of liquid being pinched in the middle and splitting the nucleus in two. But as physicists learned more about the nucleus, there were many questions that this liquid drop model did not answer. So Maria Mayer began exploring whether the nucleus might be structured as a series of concentric shells, similar to the shell-like structure of an ordinary onion.

A shell model had already been developed to explain the overall structure of the atom. Just as our solar system consists of planets that spin on their axes while orbiting the sun, this model showed electrons spinning on their axes while orbiting the nucleus of an atom. The orbital paths for electrons are called shells, and atoms of various elements have varying numbers of shells. Each shell can hold a particular number of electrons. If a shell has its maximum number, it is said to be closed. Atoms with closed electron shells are very stable and do not react readily with other elements. If a shell is not closed, however, it can share an electron from another element and form a chemical compound.

Maria Mayer theorized that protons and neutrons in a nucleus orbit in the same type of shell arrangement, but she could not prove it mathematically. Then one day, while talking to Fermi about the problem, he asked whether she had considered a property called spin-orbit coupling. With a flash of insight, she saw how this was the missing piece of the puzzle. She had failed to consider that protons and neutrons have different energies depending on whether they are spinning in the same direction in which they are orbiting or in the opposite direction. Maria compared the situation to dancers whirling around a ballroom floor, some spinning in one direction, others in the opposite direction. Those dancing a fast waltz, she said, know that spinning in one direction takes less energy than spinning in the other. By using the spin-orbit coupling theory to explain her shell model of the nucleus, Maria Mayer could explain the reason for the abnormally stable nuclei with the magic numbers. The atoms with the magic numbers had their protons and neutrons most tightly bound in their orbital shells. She published her theory in 1949. At almost the same time, German physicist Hans Jensen announced the same theory. He and Maria Mayer then collaborated on this research and published a book about it in 1955. Jensen and Mayer shared the Nobel Prize for Physics with Wigner in 1963.

In 1959, the University of California at San Diego offered both Joe and Maria Mayer full professorships with full-time salaries. The Mayers were delighted. However, Maria did not have long to enjoy this well-deserved recognition. Shortly after moving to San Diego in 1960, she suffered a severe stroke that left her with slurred speech and a paralyzed left arm. Her health steadily deteriorated, and her heart began to fail. Eventually, she required a pacemaker. But she continued to do research on nuclear physics and was able to travel to Stockholm, Sweden, in 1963 to enjoy one of the grandest parties of her life — the King of Sweden's party honoring her and other Nobel laureates. Maria Goeppert Mayer died on February 20, 1972.

BARBARA McCLINTOCK

1902-1992
Geneticist

 In grade school, Barbara McClintock was more interested in playing baseball with the neighborhood boys than she was in studying and doing homework. Although she was physically small (5 feet tall and about 90 pounds as an adult), Barbara was quite athletic and enjoyed all kinds of sports, including ice skating, tennis, volleyball, and baseball. Being the only girl on boys' teams taught her an important lesson. A girl is never quite accepted as an equal. The realization that she was "only tolerated by the boys," made Barbara spend a lot of time by herself just thinking about things. One of her greatest pleasures came from posing problems and then finding solutions, no matter how unexpected those solutions might happen to be.

Barbara McClintock's probing intellect, combined with her feisty independence, served her well when she became a scientist. She would discover that genes (the basic units of heredity) are not stable and laid out on structures called chromosomes like beads on a string. She would find that there are genetic elements that can move around and cause a variety of changes in an organism. However revolutionary McClintock's research was, she was not hailed as a visionary for her discovery of "jumping genes." Rather, it took the scientific establishment thirty years to catch up with McClintock. When other geneticists finally recognized the importance of her work, however, she was showered with awards and honors, including the 1983 Nobel Prize for Physiology or Medicine.

Barbara McClintock was born on June 16, 1902, in Hartford, Connecticut, the third of three daughters born to Dr. Thomas and Sara McClintock. She was an immediate disappointment to her parents, because they had desperately wanted a boy. The next, and last, child born to them was a boy. The family then moved to the Flatbush area of Brooklyn, New York, where Barbara's father found work as a company doctor for Standard Oil tanker crews. As the family grew, her mother was overwhelmed by caring for four children. To lighten the load and give her more time to devote to her son, Sara McClintock often sent Barbara off to stay with an aunt and uncle in rural Massachusetts. Her uncle took Barbara on his rounds as he sold fish from a horse-drawn wagon and taught her how to fix machines.

Although she and her mother were not affectionate toward one another, Barbara was not at all unhappy with her family circumstances. Both of her parents were supportive of most things that she wanted to do and gave her a great deal of freedom and independence. But, when the time came for Barbara to go to college, her mother drew the line. Sara McClintock feared that too much education would make Barbara a strange person, or worse yet, a college professor, and she did not want that.

Barbara could get no sympathy from her father, who was in France at the time, serving in the medical corps as war raged throughout Europe. So with college out of the question, Barbara took a job as an employment counselor. However, when her father returned home in 1919, he agreed to let Barbara attend Cornell University's College of Agriculture, where the tuition was free.

In her first year of college, McClintock threw herself into the school's social life. She was president of the freshmen women and played banjo with a local jazz band. She was a thoroughly modern woman who smoked, bobbed her hair, and wore knickers. However, she refused to join a sorority because they would not accept Jewish women, and many of her friends were Jewish.

As she became more absorbed in her studies, especially her graduate work in genetics, McClintock cut back on her social life. Cornell was fast becoming a major center for the science of genetics, which fascinated McClintock. At that time, scientists did not understand the chemical nature of genes. They knew that these units of heredity were located on threadlike structures called chromosomes in the cell nucleus, and that each species has a particular number of chromosomes. (For example, human beings have 46 chromosomes [23 pairs]; corn has 20 [10 pairs]; fruit flies have 8 [4 pairs].) Scientists also knew that certain genes are located on particular chromosomes, and they assumed that the positions of all genes on their chromosomes were fixed and unchanging.

In the early days of the science of genetics, there were two basic tools for studying genes — fruit flies and corn. Genetic changes, reflected for example in wing size and body or eye color, could be traced quickly through generations of fruit flies, because the flies matured and reproduced very rapidly. Maize, or Indian corn, with its multicolored kernels, was also a good genetics tool because the plant reproduces sexually, and the expression of its parent genes can be easily seen in the color and texture of each kernel. (Corn kernels are actually seeds created by the mating of male sex cells from pollen in the tassel at the tip of the plant with female sex cells in the silk at the end of each husk. Each kernel then contains one set of chromosomes from the male pollen and one from the female egg.) Genetic researchers could control corn reproduction, cross-breed plants, and observe inherited traits by growing fields of corn and selectively pollinating the plants by hand. It was through this process that McClintock, too, did her research. She grew corn and even spent nights sleeping in the cornfield to protect her plants from raccoons.

Early in her career, McClintock began making discoveries that would advance the science of genetics. While working on her master's degree, she identified each of corn's ten chromosome pairs by carefully looking for their distinct features under a microscope. McClintock determined which chromosomes carried the genes for certain traits, such as the red color of kernels or a waxy surface. Extending this work in 1931, she conducted landmark experiments with another young colleague, Harriet Creighton, that provided the first physical evidence of crossing over. (Crossing over occurs when two chromosomes physically exchange segments during meiosis, the process of cell division that sex cells undergo. Crossing over accounts for the endless variability in the traits of individuals.)

Despite her outstanding achievements, McClintock had trouble finding a job because she was a woman. After earning her doctorate in 1927, she stayed on for a while as a botany instructor at Cornell. But the university would not hire women for permanent academic positions. So she obtained several government and private research grants, which eventually took her to the California Institute of Technology, the University of Missouri, and back to Cornell University. She bought a Model A Ford and drove it cross- country from one campus to another between 1931 and 1936. During this time, she became interested in the mutations that X rays can cause. She found that when X rays break chromosomes, the chromosomes try to repair themselves. And in the process, genetic damage occurs.

In 1936, McClintock accepted her first full-time faculty position as an assistant professor at the University of Missouri. But this was not to last long. McClintock developed a reputation for being difficult to work with because she largely ignored rules. She still tended her cornfields during the summers at Cornell, and if the harvest was not ready when school began in Missouri, she came back late. She was impatient with students and others who did not understand her work. And she was outspokenly resentful about the lack of opportunity for women scientists. Because of this situation, Cornell University let McClintock know that she had no future there.

In 1941, McClintock left Cornell, vowing she would never hold another job. And, in a sense, she was able to make good on that vow. Soon after leaving Cornell, she found refuge at the Cold Spring Harbor Laboratory on Long Island, New York, where she remained for the rest of her life.

Cold Spring Harbor, operated by the Carnegie Institution of Washington, D.C., had been founded in 1890 as a center where researchers spent summers studying evolutionary theory. Gradually, it became a very prestigious, privately funded institute for basic biological research and the most important meeting ground of geneticists in the twentieth century. Eventually, McClintock was given a permanent research position there, where she could work 80 hours a week, wear blue jeans every day, and live on the grounds near her laboratory.

At Cold Spring Harbor, McClintock began the work that led to her discovery of jumping genes. She was working with corn seeds that had severely damaged ninth chromosomes. The plants that grew from these seeds had pairs of color splotches that did not correspond to hereditary patterns resulting from X-ray-caused mutations. It seemed to McClintock that something else was directing the process of trait expression. After six years of research, she came up with a possible answer. According to her theory of transposition, certain transposable elements, or jumping genes, move from one place on a chromosome to another. She described one of these elements as a gene that acts as a switch, turning other genes on and off. Another she described as an activator that causes this on-off switch to jump from one place to another on a chromosome. And this explained why she saw those odd color splotches on the corn plants. The switch had jumped next to the color gene, turning it on and off.

In 1951, McClintock gave a long, complicated presentation of her findings at a major genetics symposium. It was largely met with silence and indifference. Very few scientists could understand what she was saying. Most still supported the belief that genes could not move around. So it was not surprising that when McClintock published a paper in 1952, detailing her transposition theory, it was generally ignored outside the field of corn genetics. At first, McClintock was startled and disappointed that the scientific community did not understand her findings. But soon she was happily absorbed again in her work. "[The lack of recognition] didn't bother me," she said. "I just knew I was right." At this point, McClintock gave up on publishing her findings. Supported by private grants, she continued her work at Cold Spring Harbor, recording her results only in her personal notebooks. From 1958 to 1960, she took time off to train Latin American scientists in techniques for collecting and identifying native strains of corn.

McClintock had been honored for her earlier research. In 1944, she was elected president of the Genetics Society of America and named the third woman member of the National Academy of Sciences. Cornell University, in 1965, made her an at-large professor, and the National Academy of Sciences, in 1967, gave her its Kimber Genetics Award. In 1970, she won the National Medal of Science.

However, it was not until the new tool of molecular biology allowed researchers to probe deeper into genes that McClintock was hailed as a scientific visionary for the transposition theory she developed in the early 1950s. Molecular biologists found that genes are made of a long molecule called DNA, and they developed ways to study DNA in great detail. In the late

1960s, molecular biologists discovered transposable genetic elements in the DNA of bacteria. Then, a series of experiments with DNA in the 1970s proved that McClintock's transposition theory was true. Transposable genetic elements are now accepted as a part of life, responsible for some mutations and for the development of some diseases, perhaps even cancer. They also play an important role in genetic engineering.

After McClintock's theory was accepted and supported by the scientific community, awards and honors began pouring in. She won the highly prestigious Albert Lasker Basic Medical Research Award in 1981 and, at the age of 81, the 1983 Nobel Prize for Physiology or Medicine. Throughout her eighties, McClintock maintained a busy schedule, working twelve-hour days, getting daily exercise through aerobic dance, and twice a year visiting corn researchers in South America. Despite her rise to fame, she remained an intensely private person all her life. After only a few interviews, she refused to meet with her biographer, Evelyn Fox Keller. McClintock even refused to read the completed biography, *A Feeling for the Organism*. Although McClintock had warm relationships with family and close friends, she avoided casual associations that would take her away from her work. Her physical stamina began to wane later in life, but she was able to work on her corn research until she died on September 2, 1992.

A comment to a reporter just after Barbara McClintock had won the Nobel Prize in 1983 seems to sum up the wonderful independent spirit that saw her through difficult times in her professional life. When asked by the reporter if she was bitter about all the years she had been ignored, she answered, "If you know you're right, you don't care. You know that sooner or later, it will all come out in the wash."

MARGARET MEAD
1901-1978
Anthropologist

When Margaret Mead was eight years old, she began watching the behavior of her two younger sisters and writing down everything she observed. This activity, which may have seemed odd to outsiders, was expected behavior in the Mead home. Margaret's mother had made notes on Margaret's behavior as she was growing up. When Margaret was old enough, her paternal grandmother, a child psychologist, and her mother, a sociologist, taught her how to do the same with her sisters. And she loved doing it. Eventually, her skill at observing human behavior and her talent for recording, analyzing, and communicating what she observed, plus theorizing about it, made her a world-famous anthropologist. Her more than forty books and hundreds of commentaries on life in the South Pacific and in the United States made her a legend in her time.

Margaret Mead was born in Philadelphia, Pennsylvania, on December 16, 1901. She was one of five children born to Edward and Emily Mead. The family moved often as Edward Mead, an economics professor at the University of Pennsylvania, set up extension programs around the state. Emily Mead, a sociologist, assumed that Margaret would follow in her footsteps. But at first, Margaret wanted to be a portrait painter. And when she finally enrolled in college, it was as an English major. Apparently, however, all this changed when Margaret came under the influence of Ruth Benedict and Franz Boas, two people involved in the new science of anthropology. Their influence led her to pursue a career in anthropology.

While studying for her bachelor's degree at Barnard College, Margaret took an anthropology class taught by Franz Boas. She was fascinated by his theory of studying human civilization. He suggested that instead of digging in the ruins of prehistoric sites to determine how prehistoric people lived and behaved, scientists should observe primitive cultures currently living in remote areas of the world. This theory stayed with Mead as she completed her bachelor's degree, went on to receive a master's from Columbia University in 1924, and began earning her Ph.D. In 1929, just before receiving her Ph.D., she decided to put Boas's theory into practice and made the first of many trips to study people in the South Pacific islands.

Mead's first field trip involved studying adolescent girls living in the Pacific island chain of Samoa. Armed with notebooks and keen observation skills, she settled down in one of the villages where she learned the local language and customs and formulated conclusions that would make her name a household word before she reached the age of thirty. Her book about the experiences, *Coming of Age in Samoa* (1928), concluded that most Samoan girls do not experience the adolescent problems that American girls do. She further proposed that American girls often experience a difficult adolescence not because of physical factors but because of societal pressures. The book became a best-seller.

Until just before the beginning of World War II (1939-1945), Mead spent much of her time studying various groups living in the South Pacific. In the course of her work, she learned seven primitive languages. She described her study of New Guinea people, ranging from peaceful fishermen and artisans to fierce warriors, in her book *Growing Up in New Guinea*, published in 1930, and *Sex and Temperament in Three Primitive Societies*, published in 1935. Most of the work in the Pacific was done in collaboration with her second husband, New Zealand anthropologist Reo Fortune, whom she married in 1928. Her first marriage, in 1923, had been to Luther Cressman, a minister.

Mead was married again in 1936 to English anthropologist Gregory Bateson. During the late 1930s, she and Bateson studied societies living on Bali and in New Guinea. They returned to the United States in 1939, where Mead gave birth to a daughter, Katherine, her only child. The outbreak of war in the Pacific brought a temporary halt to Mead's field research. During

the war, she headed the Committee on Food Habits while developing strategies for helping Americans cope with food shortages. She also wrote a book about American society called *And Keep Your Powder Dry: An Anthropologist Looks at America* (1942). Influenced by Ruth Benedict's ideas of cultural determinism and the differences between male and female characteristics, Mead then wrote another book, *Male and Female*, which was published in 1949.

Following the war, Mead's life was busier than ever. She continued her work at the American Museum of Natural History in New York City. In the 1960s she organized the Hall of Pacific Peoples, which can still be seen today. It contains many artifacts from her trips to the Pacific. In 1954, she became an adjunct professor of anthropology at Columbia University, a post she held until 1978. She was also professor of anthropology and chair of the Division of Social Sciences at Fordham University from 1968 to 1970. For her contributions, Mead received many honorary degrees and awards from scientific organizations. Even after her death on November 15, 1978, she was honored with the Presidential Medal of Freedom.

Following her death, questions were raised about the reliability of her data-collecting methods. Some scientists felt that her observations and conclusions were too subjective. This served to make anthropologists aware of the difficulty of using Mead's type of observational techniques. Nevertheless, Margaret Mead will always be remembered as a major contributor to the development of cultural anthropology and the popularization of the field.

LISE MEITNER

1878-1968
Nuclear Physicist

In 1938, Lise Meitner was on the verge of making one of the greatest scientific discoveries of all time, when she had to pack up suddenly and flee for her life. Meitner, an Austrian Jewish physicist, was working at a major chemistry institute in Berlin, Germany, when Nazi leader Adolf Hitler was intensifying his persecution of Jews. Although Hitler had been in power since 1933 and had been removing Jews from influential positions, Meitner had two things to protect her — her Austrian passport and influential friends in industry who helped support the chemistry institute. At first, Meitner was allowed to continue her research, but she was banned from attending seminars, publishing articles, or giving lectures. Then the Nazis began pressuring to have her banned from the institute. She lost all protection in March 1938, when Germany invaded and annexed Austria as part of Hitler's Third Reich. She no longer had a valid passport, and the Nazi government declared that she could neither leave the country nor work.

Faced with this desperate situation, Meitner's friends arranged for her to escape by train through the Netherlands. She had to leave most of her belongings behind, including her scientific papers. For ten heart-stopping minutes near the German-Dutch border, Nazi military police boarded the train and took her passport away. But then they allowed her to cross the border to safety. They might never have let her pass had they known that Lise Meitner was soon to discover that the atomic nucleus could be split, releasing huge amounts of energy.

Lise Meitner was born in Vienna, Austria, on November 7, 1878. Hers was a large and lively family of eight children. Lise's mother was a pianist who taught music to all her children. and Lise's father was a lawyer who held very liberal views for that time. The Meitners encouraged their children to study, and four of them — two daughters and two sons — earned university degrees. One of Lise's sisters became a concert pianist.

Nevertheless, life in the late 1800s was anything but easy for young women who wanted to attend the university. In Vienna, educating girls meant giving them enough training to make them charming wives and good mothers. At age fourteen, a young woman's education came to an end because it was time to think about getting married.

But Lise wanted to study physics. Her dream of becoming a physicist seemed totally unrealistic to her family; at that time, even young men were discouraged from pursuing a physics career. The great professors believed that there was very little more to be learned, and consequently, there would be few jobs for physicists. Little did they suspect that the golden age of physics with all its discoveries about the wonders of the atom and the great forces of nature was about to dawn.

Two French scientists, Marie and Pierre Curie, were then discovering and examining elements that give off mysterious rays, which Marie Curie called radioactivity. Lise Meitner was fascinated by newspaper accounts of this. She insisted on going to the university to get a degree in science and math. Reluctantly, her father agreed. But first, he said, she must get a certificate that would qualify her to teach French so that she would have some means of supporting herself. This took three years. Then her father hired a tutor to prepare her for the university entrance exams. By the time Lise entered the university, she was twenty-three years old. In 1905, she was awarded a doctorate in physics, and soon afterward she began experiments with radioactivity, an area that was not yet of much interest to mainstream physicists.

At that time, knowledge about the atom was beginning to accumulate. The idea that matter was made up of invisible atoms had been around for centuries. In fact, the ancient Greeks had first proposed the theory of atomism in the 400s B.C. It fell out of favor during the Middle Ages, but was revived during the Renaissance in the 1500s and 1600s. By the early 1900s, modern atomic theory held that each element was made up of a particular atom and that an atom consists of a nucleus surrounded by negatively charged particles called electrons. Scientists were also coming to understand that the nucleus contains positively charged particles called protons. Nevertheless, they still thought of the nucleus as a solid little lump, not something that could be split apart. Not all physicists, however, believed there was such a thing as an atom. Lise was fortunate to have an instructor at the University of Vienna who enthusiastically endorsed the atomic theory and believed that the newly discovered radioactivity held the key to proving that atoms do indeed exist.

In the early 1900s, Berlin was considered the center for the study of physics. So Meitner applied — and was accepted — for post-doctoral study with noted physicist Max Planck at the University of Berlin. Planck was developing his quantum theory, for which he won a Nobel Prize in Physics in 1918. Planck theorized that atoms absorb and emit energy in little packets called quanta.

Meitner's determination to devote herself to the study of atomic physics so impressed her father that he gave her an allowance to live on in Berlin. Soon after arriving there, she began her long association with organic chemist Otto Hahn, who was looking for a physicist to help him with radiation experiments as he searched for new elements. But the university's chemistry institute, where Hahn's laboratory was located, would not permit women to enter the building. A compromise was reached — Meitner was allowed to carry out her radiation experiments in a basement room that had once been a carpenter's shop. In 1908, when the university officially opened its doors to women, Meitner was finally allowed upstairs.

Hahn and Meitner had a very proper working relationship. For years, they never called one another by their first names and never socialized outside the laboratory, not even to eat lunch together. Hahn chemically purified radioactive elements, and Meitner measured the radiation they gave off. The equipment they used was crude and dangerous by today's standards, and the work was tedious. Often they handled radioactive material with their bare hands. But they were making important measurements and observations that contributed greatly to the understanding of radioactive chemical elements and atomic physics. As a result, both of them became highly respected in the German scientific community.

In 1912, Meitner's career began to take off. She and Hahn moved to the new Kaiser Wilhelm Institute for Chemistry (now renamed for Max Planck) that had been funded by German industrialists. That year, Meitner also obtained her first paid position in physics when she became an assistant to Max Planck. Until that time, she had worked without pay.

When World War I (1914-1918) broke out, Meitner and Hahn were both called to serve — she as an X-ray nurse in the Austrian Army, he as a poison-gas researcher. When the war ended, they resumed their search for a new element.

The main focus of atomic research at that time was on finding or creating radioactive elements with an atomic number lower than that of uranium. An element's atomic number indicates the number of protons in the nucleus. Scientists had painstakingly worked out a Periodic Table showing the position of all the elements ranked by atomic number. Hydrogen ranked lowest of the natural elements with atomic number 1; uranium, highest at 92. In between, there were gaps in the Periodic Table and chemists were anxious to isolate these elements from natural compounds, such as uranium ore. Scientists had learned that pure uranium breaks down naturally into radioactive elements with an atomic number below 92, because the uranium nucleus changes, or decays, by losing protons. Meitner and Hahn in 1917 succeeded in isolating from uranium ore a rare radioactive element with atomic number 91, which they named protactinium.

Meanwhile, Meitner had been asked to organize a new physics department at the chemistry institute, and she became its director. The years between then and 1938 were golden ones for Meitner. Still reserved and quiet, but now filled with self-confidence, she was regarded by the institute staff as a powerful, if somewhat formal, leader. She became a highly respected researcher and counted among her friends and acquaintances such famous scientists as Max Planck, Albert Einstein, and Danish physicist Niels Bohr, who theorized that electrons circle the atomic nucleus in set orbits. Meitner's social life revolved around these great physicists, with whom she enjoyed musical evenings and going to concerts as well as attending lectures and seminars.

It was an exciting time for physicists who were finding ingenious ways to probe the atom and coming up with stunning conclusions about matter and energy. Physicists established that

radiation comes from the atomic nucleus when one atom decays, or changes into another. They discovered that the nucleus is made up of two types of particles — the neutron as well as the proton. Meitner's work was shedding light on certain types of radiation and the steps in the nuclear decay of the radioactive elements actinium, radium, and thorium. She and other nuclear scientists were also looking at the possibility of creating artificial elements with an atomic number greater than 92. They were doing this by bombarding uranium with neutrons. Soon, however, this research would take a totally unexpected turn and change the world forever.

The atom smasher, or particle accelerator, had not yet been developed, so this bombardment was done by exposing uranium to materials that give off neutrons. Neutron radiation had first been produced in 1930, when German physicist Waltner Bothe exposed the element beryllium to alpha particles — positive rays given off by radioactive elements.

In 1934, Italian physicist Enrico Fermi bombarded uranium with neutrons and thought he had created element 93. But the neutron bombardment created a bewildering array of sub-atomic particles. Meitner was fascinated by this and joined the hunt for transuranic elements — those with an atomic number higher than 92. She persuaded Hahn to join her. He brought along a young chemist, Fritz Strassman. In France, Irene Joliot-Curie was on the same quest. Yet all of these scientists were turning up some puzzling results. Interestingly, another German woman chemist — Ida Noddack — had hit upon the answer. Instead of creating bigger nuclei, she suggested they were creating smaller ones. They were splitting the uranium nucleus in two. No one, including Meitner, took this explanation seriously, however.

Hahn wondered whether they were creating radium, with atomic number 88. To test this, he and Meitner devised an experiment using nonradioactive barium to help them separate out and measure radioactive radium. They knew that radium and barium always separated out of chemical compounds together. But before she could carry out what would be one of the most important experiments in the history of physics, Meitner's career in Germany came to an abrupt end, and she fled through the Netherlands to Sweden.

Back in Germany, Hahn and Strassman continued their search for radium resulting from bombarding uranium with neutrons. And though Meitner was far from Berlin, Hahn and Strassman continued to communicate with her by mail about the puzzling results of their experiments. They could not find radium. All they could find was radioactive barium, an element with an atomic number roughly half that of uranium. What did this mean? The answer came to Meitner while she was spending the New Year's holiday with her nephew, physicist Otto Frisch, at a Swedish resort. During a walk through the snowy woods with Frisch, he recalls, she concluded that the uranium nucleus had split, forming two light elements — barium with 56 protons and krypton gas with 55 protons. Together in the woods they calculated that at the time the nucleus split, matter in the nucleus was converted into an enormous amount of energy. Frisch named the whole process nuclear fission.

A series of events then happened in rapid succession. Meitner and Frisch wrote an article about their conclusions for the British scientific journal *Nature*. But Hahn had notified a

German scientific journal about finding barium, and his article was published first. Frisch returned to his home in Copenhagen and told the story to Danish physicist Niels Bohr, who was heading off to the United States by ship. Before the *Nature* article appeared, Bohr told the exciting news to U.S. scientists, who soon saw the potential for harnessing the power of the atom. The world was at war (1939-1945), and American scientists were turning their attention to creating the ultimate weapon — the atomic bomb. They invited Meitner to collaborate on the bomb, but she refused.

Scientists working for the allies during the war collaborated on the top-secret Manhattan Project and developed the atomic bomb. On August 6, 1945, the United States dropped the first atomic bomb on Hiroshima, Japan, flattening the city and killing thousands of people. This brought an end to the war with Japan and revealed to the world the awesome drama of atomic science. Reporters swarmed to the Swedish resort town where Meitner was vacationing. They scrambled to get the views and opinions of the scientist who played such a vital role in unraveling the secrets of the atom. They were intrigued with the notion that the concepts that led to the atom bomb had been discovered by German scientists — by Meitner and by friends of Meitner who despised Hitler and withheld the secrets of atomic power from the Nazi government. Overnight, this shy and quiet scientist became world famous. She even made a transatlantic radio broadcast with the former U.S. First Lady Eleanor Roosevelt, calling for an end to war and for peaceful uses of atomic energy.

Despite Meitner's undisputed contribution, only Otto Hahn received the Nobel Prize for Chemistry in 1944, for the discovery of nuclear fission. After World War II (1939-1945), Lise Meitner refused to return to Germany where so many Jews had been exterminated by the Nazis. She spent the remaining years of her career in Sweden carrying out nuclear research, hiking, and climbing mountains. In 1960, she retired to Cambridge, England, where she died on October 27, 1968. In 1992, the artificial element 109 was named meitnerium in her honor.

Maria Mitchell

1818-1889
Astronomer

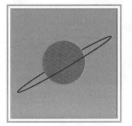

By day or by night, Maria Mitchell would climb with her father up to the widow's walk, a fenced platform on the roof of their house on Nantucket Island, Massachusetts. Together, they used simple instruments to measure the positions of the sun and other stars and check the accuracy of chronometers (timepieces) used by Nantucket whaling ships. In the 1800s, Nantucket was the world's greatest whaling port, and almost everyone who lived on the island was interested in observing the heavens and learning to navigate ships by the stars.

But the interest of Maria's father went far beyond navigation. He loved to study astronomy and became a highly respected amateur astronomer. Maria followed in his path. In 1847, she discovered a new comet. This brought her fame that was highly unusual for a woman in the mid-1800s. And even though she never had the opportunity to attend college, her skill in mathematics and astronomical observation won her the distinction of being the first professor of astronomy at the newly opened Vassar College in Poughkeepsie, New York.

Maria Mitchell was born on the island of Nantucket on August 1, 1818, the third of ten children. Her parents were devoted to learning. Her mother had worked in libraries just for the opportunity to read books, and her father became head of Nantucket's first free school in 1827. Although Maria was curious about everything, she developed a particular love for mathematics. Her intellectual curiosity was encouraged by her father. For a time, she attended his school, where the emphasis was on observing nature and learning by doing.

In 1835, at the age of seventeen, she opened her own school for girls, but the next year accepted the position of librarian at the Nantucket Atheneum, a post she held for twenty years. During this time, Mitchell used the library to further educate herself. She also continued her astronomy studies at an observatory built by her father atop the Pacific Bank where he worked. She was especially interested in the sun, but it was a comet that brought her to the attention of the world.

The king of Denmark had offered a medal for the discovery of a new comet. On the night of October 1, 1847, Maria Mitchell, using a 2-inch telescope, discovered it. This assured her reputation as a leading astronomer, and soon other honors followed. She became the first woman elected to the American Academy of Arts and Sciences in Boston in 1848 and to the new American Association for the Advancement of Science in 1850. She was hired as a computer to do calculations for the American Ephemeris and Nautical Almanac, and she helped

her father make measurements to more accurately determine longitude and latitude for the U.S. Coast Survey.

In 1857, Mitchell made the first of two journeys to Europe, where she visited observatories and met many famous people, including astronomer John Herschel, who completed the first survey of the southern sky. She made her second European trip in 1873.

Meanwhile, Mitchell had come to the attention of wealthy businessman Matthew Vassar, who was opening a women's college in Poughkeepsie, New York. At his invitation, she became Vassar's first professor of astronomy and director of the college's observatory. Her teaching methods were shockingly modern. Her method of instruction called for learning through observation, not by rote. She refused to issue grades because she said there was no intellectual unit for marking human minds, and she refused to require attendance at her classes because she believed students would attend if the teacher had any personal magnetism. In the observatory with her students she made daily photographs of sunspots on the sun's surface and observations of the surfaces of Jupiter and Saturn.

Working at Vassar reaffirmed her conviction that the popular view of women as being unsuited for mathematics and science was ridiculous. She became devoted to the cause of making higher education available to women, and in 1873, helped found the Association for the Advancement of Women, a moderate feminist group. She served as chairman of the association's science committee until her death on June 28, 1889.

WOMEN MATHEMATICIANS

Mathematics, the language of science, is an area in which the talents of women have been particularly unappreciated. Even today the myth persists that girls and women are not good at math. One sure way to dispel that myth is to look at the accomplishments of women mathematicians. Since ancient times, there have been many great women mathematicians, and there are great women mathematicians today. In fact, there was a time before electronic computers were invented when certain mathematical computations were considered "women's work." This was in the late 1800s and early 1900s, when whole departments of women mathematicians, called "computers," were set up at astronomical observatories to make the difficult and tedious calculations involved in plotting the positions and behaviors of stars and other heavenly bodies.

Many scientific concepts, especially in physics, can be understood only in terms of mathematical formulas. And women have excelled in both pure and applied mathematics. A Frenchwoman named Sophie Germain (1776-1831) came up with mathematical theories in the 1700s to explain the vibrations of elastic surfaces and also tackled the proof of a famous mathematical problem called Fermat's last theorem. Her work on the general proof of Fermat's last theorem was used by many later mathematicians. It was not until 1994 that a mathematician claimed to have finally found the proof. Yet Sophie Germain became a great mathematician without the benefit of formal education. She taught herself mathematics over the objections of her parents, who would leave her without heat or light in her bedroom and take away her clothes in an effort to stop her from studying at night. By sending mathematical papers under an assumed name to famous mathematicians, Germain caught the attention of the academic world.

In the 1800s, Russia produced the brilliant mathematician Sonya Kovalevski (1850-1891), who worked on a variety of problems, including partial differential equations and a mathematical analysis of the shape of the rings of Saturn. Kovalevski, too, had trouble getting a decent education because she was a woman. She developed an interest in mathematics literally from staring at her bedroom walls, which were papered with copies of lectures on calculus. At that time, Russian universities were closed to women, so she married a Russian geology student who was bound for school in Germany. In 1874, Kovalewski received a doctorate in mathematics from the University of Göttingen and in 1888 won a prestigious prize from the French Academy of Sciences for her paper on the rotation of a solid body around a fixed point.

The United States has produced several outstanding women mathematicians, including Anna Johnson Pell Wheeler. She was born in rural Iowa in 1883 and attended the University of South Dakota, where she met professor Alexander Pell, who encouraged her to study math. They later married. Anna went on to study mathematics at the University of Iowa, Radcliffe College, and the University of Göttingen. She received her Ph.D. in math from the University of Chicago in 1910. But as a woman, she had difficulty finding a job at the more prestigious universities. She told a friend that "there is such an objection to women that they prefer a man even if he is inferior both in training and research." Eventually, Anna Pell was hired by Bryn Mawr College, an all-women's school near Philadelphia where, after the death of her husband, she met and married Arthur L. Wheeler.

Anna Pell Wheeler, who became head of Bryn Mawr's mathematics department, was known as a fine teacher, a gifted researcher on mathematical problems involving integral equations, and an active member in professional organizations. In the 1930s, she came to the aid of another great mathematician, Emmy Noether, who was forced to flee Nazi Germany because she was Jewish.

Emmy Noether was one of the greatest mathematicians of all time. After her death in 1935, renowned physicist Albert Einstein called Noether "the most significant creative mathematical genius thus far produced since the higher education of women began." Few students have ever heard of Emmy Noether. Yet she probably has had more direct influence on daily school life than any other twentieth-century scientist or mathematician. This is because some of Noether's mathematical ideas form the foundation for what has come to be known as the "New Math."

Emmy Noether was born in Erlangen, Germany, in 1882. The Noether family was prosperous, and her father was a math professor at the University of Erlangen. Emmy shared her father's talent for and love of math, but getting an education in mathematics was almost impossible for a woman. After graduating from a school that prepared women to teach languages, Emmy began sitting in on mathematics classes at the University of Erlangen.

Before then, German universities had refused to admit women. But the first women's movement was underway, demanding the right to vote. Because of this, the world was changing. Erlangen eventually opened to women, and Noether enrolled as an official student in 1904. She was awarded a doctorate in 1907 with highest honors.

Getting an education and getting a job, however, were two different matters for women at this time. Noether managed to work at the University of Erlangen's mathematics institute — but without title or pay. Meanwhile, Noether had come to know two famous German mathematicians, David Hilbert and Felix Klein, at the University of Göttingen. They invited her to come to Göttingen, and in 1922 the university hired her and gave her the peculiar title of, "unofficial associate professor."

This was a very exciting time in both mathematics and physics. Klein and Hilbert were working with Einstein when Noether joined them. Einstein needed some new mathematical terms to express his theory of general relativity, and Noether provided some of the mathematical language for him. She also constructed a mathematical formulation called Noether's theorem, which is of major importance in quantum mechanics, the theory that predicts how sub-atomic particles and forces will behave. In the realm of pure mathematics, Noether helped develop abstract algebra. She also made important contributions to number theory, ring theory, and group representations.

Had Emmy Noether been a man, she would probably have been regarded as a lovable, eccentric, absent-minded professor. She cared nothing for money or for appearances. She was overweight, wore thick glasses, baggy dresses, sturdy oxford shoes, and a beret. Her table manners were atrocious. She has been called a female version of Albert Einstein, who also was oblivious to his clothes and surroundings. To her detractors, she was loud and crude, but her friends and students regarded her as a generous, kind-hearted human being without either malice or vanity.

The high point of Noether's career came in 1932, when she won an important mathematics prize and became the first woman to address the International Congress of Mathematics. But then life for Noether, as for all Jews in Germany, began to spiral downward. The Nazis, led by Hitler, had come to power and were beginning their campaign to eliminate Jews from positions of influence. Noether, a feminist and a left-wing liberal, was one of the first to go. In 1933, the Nazis took away her right to teach at the University of Göttingen, and Noether's friends knew she would have to leave Germany. In America, Anna Pell Wheeler invited her to teach at Bryn Mawr College. Noether accepted and spent the next two years before her death teaching undergraduates at Bryn Mawr and lecturing weekly at the Institute for Advanced Study in Princeton, New Jersey, where Einstein had taken refuge.

Noether, when she was helping with Einstein's theory of relativity, said that physics was too important to be left to the physicists. Many scientists and mathematicians might carry her sentiments a step further by saying that mathematics is too important to be left only to the male half of the human race.

Ellen Ochoa

1958-
Astronaut, Electrical Engineer

Tropical Storm Gordon was unleashing its fury of high winds and driving rain off the Florida coast on November 14, 1994. To avoid a dangerous landing, Kennedy Space Center's Mission Control directed the *Atlantis* space shuttle to touch down instead at Edwards Air Force Base in California's Mojave Desert. The alternate landing was all in a day's work for the astronauts aboard, including Ellen Ochoa, who was making her second space flight. On her first flight, in April 1993, she had become the first Hispanic American woman to orbit Earth.

Ellen Ochoa was born in Los Angeles, California, on May 10, 1958, to Rosanne and Joseph Ochoa. She and her sister and three brothers grew up in La Mesa, learning to value a good education. Her mother set a personal example by attending college herself and earning a triple major in biology, business, and journalism. When it came to academic achievement, Ellen did not disappoint her mother. An outstanding student, she excelled in math and science and also won the San Diego County spelling bee. But Ellen's interests went beyond schoolwork. She loved music and became and excellent flutist, playing in both high-school and university orchestras.

When Ellen went to college, she had a hard time deciding on a course of study. She explored music, business, computer science, and journalism, eventually earning a degree in physics from San Diego State University. She then studied electrical engineering at Stanford University, where she earned a master's degree in 1981 and a Ph.D. in 1985.

After graduating, Ochoa went to work as a research engineer at Sandia National Laboratories and obtained three patents in optical processing. She also learned how to fly a plane. When several of her friends at Stanford applied to the National Aeronautics and Space Administration for astronaut training, she applied also. But in 1988, NASA hired her as a researcher, and she quickly rose to become chief of NASA's Intelligent Systems Technology

Branch at California's Ames Research Center, Moffet Field Naval Air Station. Resuming her interest in becoming an astronaut, Ochoa meanwhile completed her training and graduated with the class of 1990.

In April 1993, she served as a mission specialist aboard the space shuttle *Discovery*, whose mission was to make observations of the sun and of Earth's atmosphere. While in orbit, Ochoa photographed the oceans and continents for future research and manipulated the shuttle's robot arm to release and later retrieve a satellite that collected data about the sun's outer layer (the corona) and the solar wind — a stream of charged particles from the sun.

In November 1994, Ochoa served as mission specialist aboard the shuttle *Atlantis*. On this mission, astronauts released a research satellite to map ozone and other gases in Earth's atmosphere. Ochoa used the shuttle's robot arm to retrieve the satellite and its instruments.

On Earth, Ochoa sees a great part of her job as being a role model for young women, especially those of Hispanic heritage. In addition to her duties of keeping up with robot arm technology and training other astronauts in its use, Ochoa travels to schools across the country giving talks on the importance of education. With a good education, Ochoa believes, a person can achieve whatever he or she wants. She takes this message to young schoolchildren who are at an impressionable age and can be influenced to go in the right direction. "I think that's where I can make a difference," she says.

RUTH PATRICK

1907-
Limnologist

 Ruth Patrick got her first microscope when she was seven years old. It was a gift from her father, a banker and lawyer whose hobby was science. Ruth's father was especially interested in looking at beautiful microscopic diatoms, single-celled algae that grow by the millions in every body of water on Earth. He passed this fascination on to his daughter who made diatoms the basis of her career as a limnologist — a scientist who studies freshwater lakes, rivers, and streams. She first learned to use diatoms as a way of detecting chemical changes that can cause pollution in water. Later, she became one of the pioneer researchers in water pollution — how to prevent it, detect it, and clean it up.

Ruth Patrick was born in Topeka, Kansas, on November 26, 1907. Her father, Frank Patrick, was a great influence on her life. Although he was a banker and lawyer, he had a degree in botany from Cornell University in Ithaca, New York, and would rather have been a scientist. He shared this love of science and nature with Ruth and her sister and took them out on Sunday afternoons to collect specimens, especially diatoms, in streams. Then he would let them look at the tiny algae under one of the four microscopes he kept at home on his roll-top desk.

There was never any question that Ruth would go to college, but where she would attend was another matter. Her mother insisted that she attend Coker College, a small women's school in Hartsford, South Carolina. Her father, worrying that Coker would not provide enough education in the sciences, arranged for Ruth to also attend summer courses at Woods Hole Oceanographic Institution on Cape Cod and at Cold Spring Harbor Laboratory on Long Island, New York. By the time Ruth graduated from Coker in 1929, she was devoted to the study of diatoms.

Patrick then enrolled at the University of Virginia in Charlottesville, where she earned a master's degree in 1931 and a Ph.D. in 1934. While in graduate school, Patrick began important work involving deposits of fossilized diatoms in strata of earth or layers of rock in the Dismal Swamp between Virginia and North Carolina. The oldest fossils are in the bottom layers, so Patrick analyzed the types of diatoms in each layer to find out how conditions in the ancient water changed over time. In the bottom layers, she found saltwater diatoms and concluded that long ago, the Dismal Swamp had been invaded by seawater, which killed off an ancient forest. Later, she did a similar study that revealed the Great Salt Lake in Utah was once a body of fresh water.

Also while in graduate school, she met and married Charles Hodge IV, an entomologist (scientist who studies insects) and a direct descendant of Benjamin Franklin. Her father made a request that was unusual for that time. He asked that Ruth retain the name Patrick when

writing scientific papers. He explained that he had always wanted to be a scientist and would like to see his name go on. During her long career, Ruth Patrick put her name on several books and more than 140 scientific papers.

After their wedding, the couple moved to Philadelphia where Charles taught zoology at Temple University. Ruth gave birth to a son and merged motherhood with her desire to work as a scientist. The country was in the grip of the Great Depression and jobs were scarce, especially for women. So she volunteered to work as a curator at the Academy of Natural Sciences, which has the largest diatom collection in the United States. Patrick remained at the Academy for her entire career, working without pay for the first ten years.

A turning point in Patrick's career came in the late 1940s, after an oil executive heard her lecture on how different diatom species flourish in different water conditions. According to Patrick, by examining diatoms, scientists could detect changes in water conditions. The oil executive was intrigued with the notion that diatoms could indicate whether a body of water had been damaged by pollution. So he raised money to investigate this possibility and insisted that Patrick head the study. Patrick did more than that. She put together teams of chemists, botanists, zoologists, and bacteriologists to examine the effects of pollution on entire water communities — groups of plant and animal species that live together in an area.

She selected Conestoga Creek in Pennsylvania for the study. Some parts of the creek were unpolluted, while others received runoff water from farm and pasturelands and industrial chemicals from factories. She and her teams discovered that pollutants kill off the most delicate species first. And in heavily polluted water, nothing lives. Thus, she was the first to prove that the health of an aquatic community indicates the degree of water pollution. And she did this more than twenty years before water pollution became a major public concern.

Ruth Patrick went on to become a leading expert on the effects of water pollution on streams and rivers. Her research took her to various parts of the United States and even to the Amazon River in South America. In 1947, she founded the Department of Limnology at the Academy of Natural Sciences. In 1952, she began teaching limnology at the University of Pennsylvania and became an adjunct professor in 1970. Acid rain became a major concern of hers, and she served on a presidential panel investigating the problem. She has also served on the boards of directors of the Pennsylvania Power and Light Company and E. I. DuPont de Nemours and Company.

During her long and distinguished career, Patrick has won many honors, including doctorates from twenty-four colleges and universities and the John and Alice Tyler Ecology Award. She was elected to the National Academy of Sciences in 1970 and to the American Philosophical Society in 1974. In 1983, on the fiftieth anniversary of her association with the Academy of Natural Sciences, the Academy renamed the laboratories of her division the Patrick Center for Environmental Research. Most recently, Ruth Patrick has received the Benjamin Franklin Medal for Distinguished Scientific Research from the American Philosophical Society.

Mary Engle Pennington

1872-1952
Chemist

People today think nothing of going to the refrigerator and pouring a glass of fresh milk or keeping fresh meat frozen for months before it is eaten. But this has only been possible since the early 1900s. Before then, people had to consume milk, eggs, and other dairy foods right away or they would spoil. They could preserve meats only by smoking or drying them. The development of frozen and refrigerated fresh foods is due in no small measure to the fact that a twelve-year-old girl named Mary Pennington read a book on medical chemistry and decided that chemistry would be her life's work.

Mary Engle Pennington, the oldest of two daughters, was born on October 8, 1872, in Nashville, Tennessee. Mary's mother and father moved to Philadelphia, Pennsylvania, soon after Mary was born to be closer to her mother's Quaker family. Mary's father was a manufacturer and an amateur gardener, and Mary loved to help him with his gardening. But her life changed when she was twelve years old and found a book in the library on medical chemistry. Her parents and her teachers were shocked when she insisted on being taught more about chemistry. In that era, there was nothing a woman could do with such knowledge. Nevertheless, they allowed her to continue, and after graduating from high school, Pennington began studying chemistry at the University of Pennsylvania in 1890.

From the beginning, she encountered sex discrimination, but she always found a way around it. By 1892, she qualified for a bachelor's degree, but the university did not bestow those on women, so they gave her a "certificate of proficiency." She just kept right on studying until she had completed her graduate work and the university finally granted her a Ph.D. in 1895. There was much to learn, because knowledge in chemistry, especially involving microorganisms, was exploding. The great French chemist Louis Pasteur had recently discovered that rapidly multiplying bacteria cause milk and other foods to spoil, and that both heat and cold slow down the growth of bacteria. In addition, Pasteur discovered that microbes are the cause of many diseases. In Germany, the physician Robert Koch had formed the theory that bacteria cause infections and infectious diseases such as tuberculosis. He was developing laboratory techniques for growing, staining, and studying bacteria. To learn all she could, Pennington earned fellowships and began postgraduate work in botany at the University of Pennsylvania and in physiological chemistry at Yale University. When she was through, she was a highly qualified chemist.

No matter what her achievements, however, Pennington found no one who would hire a woman chemist. So in 1900 she started her own business, the Philadelphia Clinical Laboratory, and analyzed medical tests for Philadelphia area physicians. She soon developed a reputation for fine work and was invited to lecture at the Women's Medical College of Pennsylvania and to head the Philadelphia Health Department's new bacteriology laboratory. There, she developed standards for milk inspection that were eventually adopted throughout the United States.

Her work caught the attention of Harvey W. Wiley, chief of the U.S. Department of Agriculture's Bureau of Chemistry and a family friend. He wanted Pennington to work for him but knew the USDA was not likely to hire a woman. So he suggested that she take the civil service test under the name M. E. Pennington. She passed, of course, and was hired as a bacteriologist before anyone found out that M. E. Pennington was a woman. In 1908, Wiley appointed her head of the USDA Food Research Laboratory, established to help enforce the Pure Food and Drug Act of 1906.

Pennington and her staff, which eventually numbered fifty-five, investigated various food-processing industries, developed refrigeration techniques and other methods for preventing the spoilage of eggs, poultry, and fish, and helped devise techniques for packaging and storing foods. Even when stored in cold temperatures, food will spoil after a time by breaking down chemically from the growth of bacteria and the poisons that some bacteria give off. And if there is too much moisture in the storage area, mold will grow on foods. Pennington and her staff worked on finding ways to keep food fresh for the longest time.

During World War I (1914-1918), Pennington investigated refrigerated railroad cars for transporting food, riding in the caboose and checking the temperature of the cars at regular intervals. She established the first standards for building and operating refrigerated cars designed to carry food. For her work on perishable foods, she earned a Notable Service Medal.

She left the USDA in 1919 and moved to New York City to head the research and development department of American Balsam, a manufacturer of insulating materials. But in 1922, she again went out on her own, this time as a consultant. Her work with packing houses, shipping companies, and warehousing firms greatly influenced the food preservation industry. Gradually, it led her to an interest in freezing as a way of preserving food. In the 1920s, Clarence Birdseye developed a quick-freezing method that would make frozen food a staple in the American diet. Nevertheless, there were

many issues surrounding freezing, such as how to create packaging that would seal in moisture and prevent freezer burn, and how best to prepare various types of foods for freezing. Pennington did research on these things and published the results of her work in both business and government journals.

In her lifetime, Pennington belonged to many scientific and industrial organizations and was the first woman member of the American Society of Refrigerating Engineers. She was still working and serving as vice president of the American Institute of Refrigeration when she died on December 27, 1952.

Judith Graham Pool

1919-1975
Physiologist

People with the blood disorder known as hemophilia owe a great deal to the work of Judith Pool. Until her important discoveries, this inherited illness caused untold suffering. Hemophilia is a genetic disorder that affects mainly males. Because the blood of hemophiliacs does not clot properly, they can bleed excessively from even the smallest cut. But internal bleeding into the joints is far more serious. In addition to being extremely painful, repeated bleeding in the joints can cause crippling. The disease occurs when one of the substances that causes blood to clot is missing. The work of Judith Graham Pool revolutionized the treatment of hemophilia by making the missing clotting factor widely available. Thanks to her research, hemophiliacs can now inject themselves with the normal clotting factor and lead relatively normal lives.

Judith Graham was born on June 1, 1919, in Queens, New York, the oldest of three children. Her father was a stockbroker; her mother, a schoolteacher. After graduating from high school, Judith attended the University of Chicago, where she met and married Ithiel de Sola Pool, a graduate student in political science. After earning a bachelor of science degree in 1939, Judith continued her graduate work. In 1942 the Pools moved to Geneva, New York, to teach at Hobart and William Smith Colleges.

The same year, while working on her Ph.D. at the University of Chicago with neurophysiologist Ralph Waldo Gerard, Judith Pool developed a microelectrode for measuring electrical activity in a single cell. She used this tool to determine the electrical potential of a single muscle fiber membrane. Science historians believe that the microelectrode was first invented in 1921 by physiologist Ida H. Hyde, although the discovery was lost until the 1940s. As a result, Gerard is commonly given credit for its discovery and was even nominated for a Nobel Prize.

After earning a Ph.D. in 1946, Pool did little in the way of research, devoting her time to her two sons, and her husband's career. But in 1948, when her husband accepted a position at Stanford University's Hoover Institution on War, Revolution, and Peace, the family moved to California. There, Judith Pool's career blossomed.

In 1950, she became a research assistant at the Stanford Research Institute and in 1953 a research fellow at Stanford's School of Medicine, where she began her landmark work on how blood coagulates. She developed a way to separate the antihemophiliac clotting factor, called factor VIII, from blood plasma. Her method of cold precipitation of factor VIII, announced in 1964, became the standard for making transfusions of factor VIII, which hemophiliacs take whenever they injure themselves or detect internal bleeding.

During this period, Pool made time for a third child — a daughter born in 1964. By 1972 she was divorced from her first husband and had married Maurice Sokolow, a blood specialist. Three years later, they too were divorced.

On July 13, 1975, Judith Pool died of a brain tumor, just a few years before the deadly disease AIDS made its appearance. She would never know that some of the donated blood from which factor VIII was isolated had become contaminated with the virus that causes AIDS. As a result, many hemophiliacs contracted AIDS after being injected with contaminated factor VIII. Today, however, donated blood is routinely tested for the AIDS virus and factor VIII transfusions are once again safe.

During her lifetime, Judith Graham Pool received recognition and many honors for her important work. Unlike most women scientists, however, Judith Pool felt overrewarded and overrecognized. Stanford promoted her to senior research associate in 1956, senior scientist in 1970, and full professor in 1972. The National Hemophilia Foundation renamed its fellowship awards the Judith Graham Pool Research Fellowships.

Judith A. Resnick

1949-1986
Astronaut, Electrical Engineer

She was a very quiet girl but always had the right answer when called upon in school. Determination, combined with talent in science and mathematics, eventually won for Judith Resnik the distinction of becoming one of the first six women selected in 1978 by the National Astronautics and Space Administration to train as astronauts.

Judith Arlene Resnik (her friends called her J.R.) was born on April 5, 1949, in Akron, Ohio. As a youngster, Judith diligently practiced the piano for an hour every day. In high school, she was a member of the chemistry and French clubs and the only female member of the math club. When it was time for college, she chose Carnegie-Mellon University in Philadelphia, from which she received a B.S. in electrical engineering in 1970.

Resnik then went to work for the RCA Corporation in Moorestown, New Jersey, where she helped develop circuits for radar control systems. She continued her education at the University of Maryland, receiving a Ph.D. in electrical engineering in 1977. After graduating, she was hired by the Xerox Corporation in El Segundo, California, as a senior systems engineer for product development. But when she heard NASA was opening its astronaut program to women, she applied for admission.

Realizing the competition would be fierce, Resnik began to train. She ran every day to build up her endurance. Meanwhile, she did research on NASA at the Air and Space Museum in Washington, D.C., and learned to fly. Her determination paid off. In 1978, she, Sally Ride, Rhea Seddon, Anna Fisher, Shannon Lucid, and Kathryn Sullivan were selected from among 8,000 applicants, including 1,000 women, to train as astronauts.

Resnik and the five other women trained vigourously as mission specialists, scientists, and technicians whose responsibilities would include handling experiments and deploying satellites. In addition to physical training, Resnik worked with Sally Ride, the first American woman to fly in space, on developing the remote manipulator arm to launch satellites from the shuttle's cargo bay and also recapture orbiting satellites for repair.

On August 30, 1984, Resnik became the second American woman in space when the space shuttle *Discovery* lifted off with a crew of six on its first voyage. The crew launched a communications satellite and tested a solar array — a wing of solar cells that convert sunlight into electricity. *Discovery* touched down safely on September 5, with Resnik having logged a total of 144 hours, 57 minutes in space.

Resnik's next mission was set for January 28, 1986, aboard the *Challenger*. It was a special mission, because for the first time, a civilian would be on board — science teacher Christa McAuliffe. Just before the launch, the weather in Florida was unusually cold. The temperature had dipped to 36° F. No space shuttle launch had ever been attempted in temperatures this cold.

When the seven-member crew, including Resnik and McAuliffe, boarded the shuttle, everything appeared to be normal. But 73 seconds after liftoff, the *Challenger* exploded, killing everyone aboard. On that fateful day, Judith Resnik became the first woman astronaut to die in the line of duty.

In the wake of the tragedy, a twelve-member presidential commission was formed to look into the cause of the disaster. The commission determined that the explosion was due to faulty booster rocket design and to the cold weather's effect on an O-ring — a rubber ring that provides a seal between the sections of the booster rockets. Because the O-ring failed to hold in the searing exhaust of liftoff, gas burned through the main fuel tank, resulting in the fatal explosion. After the *Challenger* disaster, the space shuttle was redesigned.

ELLEN HENRIETTA SWALLOW RICHARDS

1842-1911
Chemist and Environmental Engineer

Ellen Swallow Richards was a practical person. She grew up on a farm in the 1800s, helping her father with chores and her mother with housework. When her family moved to town and her father opened a store, she helped there, too, learning about the economics of buying and selling. Later, when she wanted higher education and her parents did not have the means to pay for it, Ellen taught school, cleaned other people's houses, and did whatever it took to earn tuition money. But in addition to being a practical, problem-solving person, she also had a gift for seeing things in new ways. Once her science career was well underway, she applied science to solving society's problems of polluted air and water, crowded cities, and malnourished families. She was one of the first to see the human environment as a series of interconnected life systems. By recognizing the importance of pure water, clean air, and uncontaminated food, she became one of the first environmental scientists. Today, some people regard her as the founder of ecology.

Ellen Henrietta Swallow was born on December 3, 1842, in Dunstable, Massachusetts. Both of her parents taught school. Her father also owned a farm and later village stores in Westford and Littleton, Massachusetts. After being taught by her parents at home, Ellen entered Westford Academy and then a school in Worcester. She was determined to obtain a higher education, but she ran up against some very large obstacles. The first was the fact that few colleges accepted women. The second was financial. Ellen Swallow was not afraid of hard work and took on a series of jobs teaching, cleaning, cooking, nursing, and working in the family store to save for college. By 1868, she had saved about $300 — enough money to enroll in Vassar College in Poughkeepsie, New York. By then, she was twenty-five years old. Vassar admitted her to the senior class the following year.

At Vassar, she was privileged to study with the famous astronomer, Maria Mitchell, and chemistry professor Charles A. Farr, who believed that science should be applied to solve practical problems. At first Ellen Swallow intended to became an astronomer, but chemistry won out. After graduating from Vassar in 1870, she headed for the Massachusetts Institute of Technology, founded only five years before. To her delight, she was admitted as a special student in chemistry, and without charge. She had thought this was because of her financial situation, but later learned that by not charging her the president could claim she was not a student should anyone object to the presence of a woman at M.I.T. When she discovered this, she was furious and said that if she had known, she would never have entered M.I.T.

Swallow's first environmental study — a chemical analysis of water supplies — was carried out while she was still a student at M.I.T and an assistant to a professor who was analyzing water supplies for the Massachusetts Board of Health. Her work helped establish the first state standards for water purity.

In 1873, Swallow learned chemical analysis of minerals while studying with Robert H. Richards, head of M.I.T.'s metallurgical laboratory. They were opposites in every way. He was handsome and slow to act. She was rather plain and quick in thought and action. Proving that opposites attract, Richards proposed to her in the chemistry lab. She accepted, and they were married in 1875. They had no children and devoted themselves to supporting each other's scientific efforts.

Marriage gave Ellen Richards financial security and allowed her to devote her energies to science. She helped Robert with the chemical aspects of his metallurgical work. She became an expert in a number of fields, from the chemical analysis of water, air, and minerals to the analysis of food and nutritional requirements. Deeply concerned about the environment, Richards wrote a prophetic letter to the president of M.I.T in the early 1900s. "One of the most serious problems of civilization," she said, "is clean water and clean air, not only for ourselves but for the world."

Richards spent her entire career at M.I.T. From 1875 until 1883, she concentrated on scientific education for women. She established the Women's Laboratory at M.I.T. and helped teach female students chemical analysis, industrial chemistry, biology, mineralogy, health, and finances. In addition, she undertook projects for government and private industry, which included testing for arsenic in fabrics and wallcoverings, looking for adulterations in staple food products, and exploring the causes of spontaneous combustion. She also developed science courses for the Society to Encourage Studies at Home, a private correspondence school for women.

Richards personally corresponded with her students and learned about the illnesses that plagued middle-class women, many of which were caused by social conventions of the day. For example, fashion dictated that women in the late 1800s lace themselves into tight-fitting corsets that made breathing difficult. As a result, some women fainted from lack of oxygen after the slightest exertion. So Richards wrote a pamphlet explaining how to dress, eat, and exercise for good health. She

also was a founder of what became known as the American Association of University Women, whose first goal was to dispel the myth that too much learning was detrimental to a woman's health.

At M.I.T., Richards advised the students in the Women's Laboratory to conduct themselves with discretion. Her goal was to see that women were admitted into regular degree programs. Her strategy to achieve this goal was to steer clear of feminist politics, which at the time centered around voting rights for women. Her strategy worked when women became full-fledged M.I.T. students and the Women's Laboratory closed in 1883.

In 1884, Richards became an instructor of sanitary chemistry in M.I.T.'s new chemical laboratory. She carried out the first major analysis of the state's entire water supply, and then spent the next twenty-seven years teaching classes in the techniques of analyzing air, sewage, and water. She also helped found the Seaside Laboratory for the study of ocean and inland waters, which became the famous Marine Biological Laboratory at Woods Hole.

Convinced that one's home is the first place to begin improving the human environment, Richards turned her own home into a laboratory where she installed such innovations as a hot-water heater, shower, and ventilation system. In 1892, she called for the establishment of a new science to be named *oekology* (the Greek word for "household"), which would encompass nutritional issues for consumers as well as education about the environment.

Richards soon found herself in charge of the nutrition-consumer branch, which became the home economics movement, a very practical approach to educating women about the scientific basis for nutrition and sanitation. She helped found the American Home Economics Association and the *Journal of Home Economics*. While educating women about healthful living at home, she was also teaching chemical sanitation techniques to many of the men who went on to develop municipal water-treatment and sewage facilities. Public health experts credit the development of better sanitation to the increased life expectancy of Americans — from forty-seven years in 1900 to seventy-five by the mid-1990s. Richards remained at M.I.T. until her death from a heart attack on March 30, 1911.

SALLY KRISTEN RIDE

1951-
Astronaut and Astrophysicist

As a teenager, Sally Ride was torn between two worlds — the world of science and the world of sports. She was a born athlete, and even the likes of women's tennis star Billie Jean King advised her to make a career of the game. But eventually science won out. Ride became a Ph.D. astrophysicist and entered the U.S. astronaut-training program. In 1983, she catapulted to fame as the first American woman in space.

Sally Kristen Ride was born in Los Angeles, California, on May 26, 1951. Her father, Dale Ride, was a professor of political science. Her mother, Carol, later worked as a volunteer in a women's prison. The Rides never pressured their two daughters to follow a particular course in life but did encourage them to do their best in school.

At first, Sally cared much more about sports than she did about her studies. She loved to play baseball and football with the boys in the neighborhood. In 1961, the year the United States launched its first astronaut into space, Sally Ride took up tennis. Soon she was playing on the junior tennis circuit and won a tennis scholarship to a private prep school for girls. It was there that she had her first close encounter with science.

Ride came under the influence of Dr. Elizabeth Mommaerts, an inspiring teacher of physiology. From then on, science was a serious contender for Ride's attention. In 1968, she began her college career at Swarthmore as a physics major, only to drop out and take up tennis again. Ride returned to college in 1970, this time at Stanford University, where she studied both English and physics. Ride developed a deep love of Shakespeare, and after graduating in 1973 with a B.S. in physics and a B.A. in English, she considered making Shakespeare the focus of her graduate studies. But once again, science won out, and Ride began studying to be an astrophysicist, a scientist who studies the physical properties of stars and other objects in the sky. Her graduate studies included work in X-ray astronomy and in high-energy lasers. She earned her Ph.D degree in 1978.

Ride claimed she had no great plans to become an astronaut. In fact, she never even thought it was possible. ". . .When I saw [astronauts] on TV they all seemed to be Navy or Air Force test pilots," she told a newspaper reporter, "I suppose I just took it for granted that it was pretty much a closed club."

The National Aeronautics and Space Administration's astronaut training program during its first twenty years *was* a closed club — and definitely closed to women. But with the development of the space shuttle, NASA needed scientists as well as test pilots to fly into space and handle complex experiments. (The astronaut-scientists are called mission specialists.)

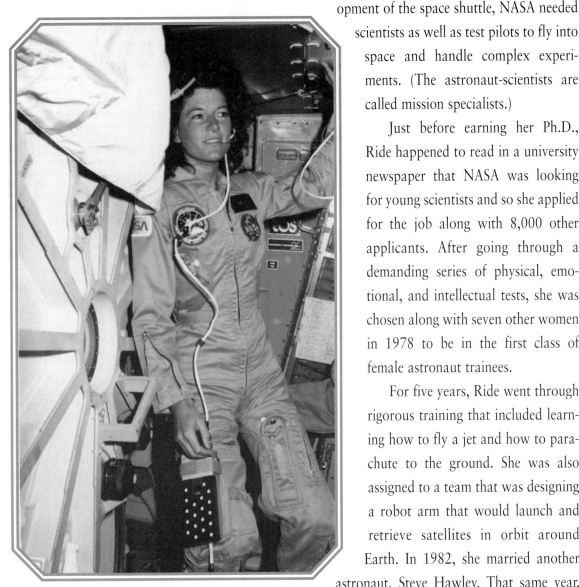

Just before earning her Ph.D., Ride happened to read in a university newspaper that NASA was looking for young scientists and so she applied for the job along with 8,000 other applicants. After going through a demanding series of physical, emotional, and intellectual tests, she was chosen along with seven other women in 1978 to be in the first class of female astronaut trainees.

For five years, Ride went through rigorous training that included learning how to fly a jet and how to parachute to the ground. She was also assigned to a team that was designing a robot arm that would launch and retrieve satellites in orbit around Earth. In 1982, she married another astronaut, Steve Hawley. That same year,

Navy Captain Robert L. Crippen chose Ride for a space shuttle mission that would try out the remote mechanical manipulator arm for the first time.

On June 18, 1983, the space shuttle *Challenger* roared off its launch pad at Cape Canaveral, Florida, carrying Ride into history. During the six-day space flight, Ride helped launch Canadian and Indonesian communications satellites and successfully tested the ability of the robot arm to launch and retrieve satellites. After returning to Earth, Ride said in an interview: "The thing I'll remember most about the flight is that it was fun. In fact, I'm sure it was the most fun that I'll ever have in my life." Ride made a second space flight in 1984 to launch a research satellite for studying the effect of the sun on weather.

Then tragedy touched her life and the lives of all the astronauts and their families on January 28, 1986, when the space shuttle *Challenger* exploded shortly after liftoff. Ride was appointed to head a special presidential commission to look into the causes of the explosion, which was later traced to a faulty O-ring that served as a seal between sections of the booster rockets and prevented hot gases from escaping.

In 1987, Sally Ride resigned from NASA and became a science fellow at Stanford University. Then in 1989 she became a professor of physics at the University of California at San Diego and director of the university's California Space Institute.

VERA COOPER RUBIN

1928-
Astronomer

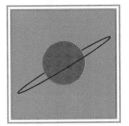

Vera Cooper Rubin has always been obsessed with the stars. As a young girl, she watched the progression of the constellations around the North Star in the night sky from her bedroom window — sometimes all night long. As an adult astronomer, her interest expanded to encompass the vast islands of stars in the universe called galaxies. She has spent many nights at gigantic telescopes on mountains in North and South America, focusing intently on areas of particular interest and capturing them on photographic plates. She has spent long days over a microscope, painstakingly studying the thousands of tiny lines or bands on a photograph that represent the pattern of light from a galaxy. Her analysis and calculations have led her to conclude that things do not add up in intergalactic space. Something is missing. And this missing "something" has turned out to be the greatest mystery about our universe facing astronomers and cosmologists today.

Vera Cooper was born on July 23, 1928, in Philadelphia, Pennsylvania. When she was ten years old, the family moved to Washington, D.C. Both of her parents strongly favored education for women, because they believed a woman should be able to support herself. Vera's father, an engineer, encouraged her interest in mathematics and astronomy and helped her build a telescope when she was fourteen years old.

When it came time for Vera to select a college, she applied to Swarthmore, where she wanted to major in astronomy. But when an admissions officer suggested she might be better off in a more ladylike occupation, such as painting heavenly objects, Vera went to Vassar College instead. Vassar, in Poughkeepsie, New York, had an excellent tradition of astronomical education for women, beginning with its first astronomy professor, Maria Mitchell.

After graduating from Vassar in 1948, Cooper applied to Princeton University, a renowned center for astrophysical studies. However, Princeton had a strict policy of not accepting women. In fact, it was not until 1971 that the first woman was allowed into

Princeton's graduate astrophysics program. So Vera applied to Harvard University in Cambridge, Massachusetts, instead. Although she had won a scholarship to Harvard and had applied for admission, she never actually attended the school.

As was the tradition for young women in the late 1940s, Vera married immediately after graduating from college. By her own admission, she was very conventional and wanted a family. Neither she nor her husband Robert Rubin considered going anywhere but to Cornell University in Ithaca, New York, where Robert was pursuing graduate studies in chemistry. Although Cornell had a very small — and not very prestigious — astronomy department, Vera eventually obtained her a master's degree in astronomy from Cornell in 1951. This is when she had her first brush with scientific controversy.

By the 1950s, astronomers had built very powerful telescopes for seeing vast distances into space and sensitive spectrographs for analyzing light coming from distant corners of the universe. As a result, they had learned that the universe is populated with millions of galaxies containing billions of stars. They had also concluded that the universe has been expanding ever since the "big bang," when space and time exploded into being. They had come to this conclusion by studying a phenomenon known as redshift.

Redshift occurs when light waves are stretched or shifted to the longer-wavelength red end of the spectrum. This is a result of the Doppler effect, the stretching or compressing of waves, such as sound or light. We can hear the Doppler effect in the whistle of a train or the wail of an ambulance siren. As the sound moves toward us, the waves are compressed. The sound changes as the ambulance or train passes us and moves away, because the sound waves are then stretched out. Similarly, the light waves from an object in space moving away from Earth are stretched out toward the red end of the spectrum and the light waves from an object moving toward Earth are compressed or shifted toward the blue end of the spectrum. This redshift or blueshift is a powerful tool that astronomers use for measuring how fast stars and galaxies are moving and how far away they are from our solar system.

Vera Rubin used redshift measurements for her master's thesis, suggesting that if the planets in our solar system orbit the sun, which is a star, and the stars in a galaxy orbit its center, then might not all the galaxies in the universe be orbiting around something too? The controversial idea received a great deal of publicity in the scientific community and in the press. But no one believed it.

Soon afterward, her husband obtained a job in Washington, D.C., where they moved with their new baby, David. Vera settled down to being a wife and mother. But something was missing from her life. Every time the *Astrophysical Journal* arrived in the mail, she would sit down and cry. Knowing how much she wanted to become an astronomer, she enrolled in the Ph.D. program at Georgetown University. While she took night classes, her mother took care of David and then Judith, who was born in 1952. Vera made sandwiches for Robert, who drove her to class and ate his supper while he waited for her in the car. All their sacrifices paid off. In 1954, Vera Rubin was awarded a Ph.D. in astronomy for her thesis on the distribution of galaxies throughout space.

From 1954 through 1965, Vera Rubin taught at Georgetown University and gave birth to two more children, Karl and Allen. Eventually, all her children received their Ph.D.s in science or mathematics.

In 1965, Rubin accepted a post as a part-time astronomer with the Carnegie Institution of Washington, D.C., and returned to the problem she set forth in her master's thesis. Again, her idea that the galaxies themselves were rotating about some kind of center stirred controversy, which Rubin found to be very unpleasant. Most astronomers believed that the universe had been smoothly expanding since the big bang. Because this theory did not allow for any clumps of matter or for any peculiar motions outside the general expansion, she was urged to abandon her research. But Rubin was on the right track. Astronomers have since discovered that the galaxies are moving toward something they call the Great Attractor.

To avoid further controversy, Rubin turned her research to what she thought was a fairly mundane topic — the motion of spiral galaxies. Spiral galaxies are great collections of stars, dust, and gas organized as a central bulge surrounded by a rotating disk. But spirals also have arms extending from the disk, like pinwheels in intergalactic space.

Like all heavenly bodies, the stars in galaxies are held in position by the force of gravity. Gravity holds the planets in orbit around the sun, and holds the stars in place as they rotate about the galaxy's central core. Astronomers had assumed that most of the matter in a galaxy is concentrated in its brightly shining core, or central bulge, just as most of the matter in our solar system is concentrated in the center around the sun and inner planets. One result of this concentration of matter is that the inner planets travel faster than outer planets as they orbit the sun. So astronomers assumed that the same was true of galaxies. The stars near the center would move faster than the stars at the edge of the galaxy. What a surprise when Vera Rubin discovered that this was not true.

Working with physicist W. Kent Ford, a designer of sensitive astronomical instruments, Rubin competed for observing time at Kitt Peak Observatory in Arizona and other large telescopes. First she studied Andromeda, the closest spiral galaxy. By painstakingly examining the redshift and blueshift of stars and gas clouds at all positions in Andromeda, Rubin came up with the startling observation that all the stars and gas were moving at the same speed, no matter whether they were close to the center or far away. She and a team of astronomers at Carnegie came up with the same results for other galaxies also. There could be only one explanation for this: there is more matter in a galaxy than is visible to even the most powerful telescopes. In fact, astronomers have concluded that as much as 90 percent of the matter in the universe is invisible. They now call this missing mass dark matter. For her accomplishments, including her contribution to this discovery, Rubin was awarded the National Medal of Science in 1993.

Astronomers and astrophysicists are now embroiled in controversial debate over what this dark matter might be. Some think it consists of cold, dark bodies the size of the planet Jupiter. Others believe it is more likely to be bizarre subatomic particles created at the very birth of the universe. Cosmologists are anxious to solve this mystery because the answer may tell us the ultimate fate of the universe. If there is a certain critical amount of mass, the universe will someday stop expanding and begin falling back in on itself, ending up in what has been dubbed "the big crunch." If there is not enough matter to stop the expansion, the galaxies will continue to move farther and farther apart until, billions of years from now, the universe will grow cold and the light of the stars will burn out.

Vera Rubin's work did much to bring this great mystery to the fore. But it will probably be left to the next generation of astronomers to work out its solution. "With over 90 percent of the matter in the universe still to play with," Vera Cooper Rubin says, "even the sky will not be the limit."

Florence Rena Sabin

1871-1953
Anatomist

 At the U.S. Capitol Building in Washington, D.C., every state in the Union is allowed to display the statues of two of its most distinguished citizens in Statuary Hall. The state of Colorado chose for one of its statues the likeness of Florence Sabin, an outstanding medical scientist who achieved an impressive number of "firsts" for women. She was the first woman on the Johns Hopkins Medical School faculty in Baltimore, Maryland; the first woman member of the Rockefeller Institute; and the first woman elected to the National Academy of Sciences. Sabin had not one, but three distinguished careers, first as a researcher and teacher at Johns Hopkins, then as a researcher of tuberculosis at the Rockefeller Institute. Her third career began after she retired. She overhauled the state public health system of Colorado and, at age seventy-six became head of Denver's new city health department.

Florence Rena Sabin was born in Central City, Colorado, on November 9, 1871, the youngest of two daughters born to Serina and George Sabin. At that time, mining was a booming business in Colorado, where Florence's father worked as a mining engineer. After his wife's death, George could not cope with raising two daughters, so he sent Florence, then four years old, and her sister Mary to Wolfe Hall boarding school in Denver. A short time later, George's brother, Albert Sabin, brought the girls to Chicago, Illinois, where they could be part of a family. These were four of the most happy and intellectually stimulating years for Florence. When she was twelve years old, she went to live with her grandparents on their farm in Vermont and eventually enrolled at Smith College in 1889.

While at Smith College, Sabin developed two great interests — medicine and women's rights. She actively worked for passage of laws giving women the right to vote and decided to go to medical school to become a doctor. After graduating in 1893, Sabin taught two years at Wolfe Hall in Denver and a year in the zoology department at Smith. With the money she had saved, she applied to Johns Hopkins Medical School. This was her best bet, because the school had been funded by a group of women who insisted that women be admitted on the same basis as men. She was admitted and began making lasting contributions even while she was a student. Her abilities and enthusiasm so impressed anatomy professor Franklin P. Mall that he encouraged her to create a model of the brain. This work, which she undertook as a student, was published in 1901 as *An Atlas of the Medulla and Midbrain*, and became a popular text for medical students.

After earning her M.D. in 1900, Sabin served a one-year internship and then began a research and teaching career at Johns Hopkins that eventually spanned twenty-five years. Beginning with a fellowship, Sabin became an assistant in anatomy, an associate professor in

1905, and a full professor in 1917. When Franklin Mall, chairman of the anatomy department, retired, Sabin expected to replace him, but a man was appointed instead. When colleagues asked whether she would resign in protest, Sabin replied, "Of course I'll stay. I have research in progress."

Her particular interest was the development of the blood cells and the lymphatic system. In the early 1900s, scientists were just beginning to learn how organs, tissues, and systems develop in the body. Sabin spent untold hours peering into a microscope at blood cells and blood vessels. By injecting the vessels in pig embryos with India ink and tracing them, she learned that the lymph vessels grow from veins in the early stages of development. Lymph vessels are similar to blood vessels, but they collect fluid that seeps out of tiny blood vessels and return the fluid to the bloodstream.

Sabin also believed that research should aid in medical education. She held that a good teacher had to be a good researcher and encouraged her students to find answers by conducting experiments rather than just reading textbooks. Many of her students went on to become famous researchers themselves.

In 1925, she went to work as a scientist at the Rockefeller Institute, now Rockefeller University. She took on the study of tuberculosis, a major public health scourge at the time. Now, tuberculosis is treated with antibiotics, but in the 1920s these drugs did not exist. Sabin headed a team that studied how the body's disease-fighting immune system reacts to the bacterium that causes TB. After a long and distinguished research career, Sabin retired in 1938. She had accumulated many awards and honors. In addition to being elected to the National Academy of Sciences in 1925, she had served as the first woman president of the American Association of Anatomists from 1924-1926 and in 1921 had been selected to represent women scientists by welcoming the great French physicist Marie Curie when she visited the United States. So Sabin had behind her a lifetime of achievements of which she could be proud when she returned to Denver to live quietly with her sister.

But that was just the beginning of the Florence Sabin story. Sabin became interested in public health matters during World War II (1939-1945). In 1944, the governor of Colorado invited Sabin to serve on a postwar planning committee for reintegrating servicemen into civilian life and to head a subcommittee on public health. The governor apparently appointed Sabin not so much because of her reputation as a researcher but because he had been assured that she was a nice old lady with her hair in a bun who knew little of life outside the laboratory. How wrong that assessment proved to be.

Florence Rena Sabin found that Colorado's public health system was inefficient, corrupt, and hampered by untrained staff and insufficient funding. She publicized these shocking findings and campaigned across the state for laws and other reforms to control infectious disease, ensure the purity of milk, and allow for sanitary sewage disposal. Her committee drafted new health laws known as the Sabin Program and worked successfully for their adoption by the state legislature.

In 1947, the mayor of Denver appointed Sabin manager of the city's Board of Health and Hospitals, a post she held until 1951. That year she was honored with the Lasker Award, the most prestigious honor in medical science. She finally retired for good at the age of eighty and died of a heart attack two years later on October 3, 1953.

NETTIE MARIA STEVENS

1861-1912
Biologist

No one is certain when Nettie Stevens first peered into the eyepiece of a microscope and saw a wonderful secret world of strange-looking, one-celled animals swimming in a single drop of water on a glass slide. But whatever she felt at that moment motivated her to learn more about the secrets of the microscopic world. Even though circumstances prevented her from beginning a college degree program until she was thirty-five years old, and her professional research career spanned only nine years, Nettie Maria Stevens made up for lost time. She made a discovery that led to an understanding of how sex is determined in an organism.

Nettie Maria Stevens was born in Cavendish, Vermont, on July 7, 1861. When she was two years old, her mother died and her father, a carpenter, remarried. Other than that, historians know little about young Nettie's early life. She received her education at public schools in Westford, Massachusetts, and at Westford Normal School, where teachers were trained. She then worked as a teacher and a librarian in various Massachusetts towns from 1883 to 1896.

Teaching, nursing, and secretarial work were among the few occupations open to women at that time. Most universities would not even accept women as students. So when Nettie Marie Stevens saw an opportunity for more education, she took it. Hearing that Stanford University in California was accepting women scholars, she enrolled in 1897. She earned a bachelor's degree in 1899 and a master's degree a year later. Then she entered the Ph.D. program at Bryn Mawr College in Pennsylvania, a women's college that had recently opened.

Even before she finished her Ph. D., Stevens was distinguishing herself as a researcher in the microscopic study of the structure and function of one-celled animals called protozoa. She also did research involving the development of embryos in lower life forms. She was awarded fellowships to study in Naples, Italy, and Wurzberg, Germany. After earning her Ph.D. in 1903, she remained at Bryn Mawr where she began researching how sex is determined.

At Bryn Mawr, Stevens studied and worked with well-known biologists Thomas H. Morgan and Edmund B. Wilson. Both were fascinated with the work of an Austrian monk named Gregor Mendel who, while working with pea plants in the 1860s, had determined the rules by which traits, such as color and size, are passed from parents to offspring. He theorized that the traits were transmitted by some unknown hereditary factors. Mendel's work had been lost until 1900, but with its rediscovery, biologists were interested in looking for these hereditary factors.

Using a microscope, scientists already had observed the tiny threadlike structures that become visible inside the nucleus of a cell when it divides. They called these structures chromosomes and wondered whether they were Mendel's hereditary factors. It seemed unlikely, they thought, because there were few chromosomes in relation to the number of traits. The number of chromosomes varied from one species to another, some having only ten or twenty while human beings had forty-six. But even this was too few to account for the hundreds of traits that scientists had already categorized.

Like most biologists of the time, Stevens and Morgan at first believed that sex was determined by external factors such as temperature or food the mother ate. Therefore, initially, their study was designed to find out which of the external factors was most important. But, like many scientific experiments, the results turned out to be far different than expected.

After obtaining a grant from the Carnegie Institute, Stevens began her research by observing the sex cells of insects under a microscope. She noticed something that turned out to be of major importance. The unfertilized female sex cell, or egg, contained two of the large X chromosomes. The male cell, or sperm, however, contained either one X or one smaller Y chromosome. Working with the sex cells of a species of beetle, Stevens correctly concluded that sex is determined by specific combinations of chromosomes from egg and sperm. Geneticists eventually learned that the sex cells divide so that they contain only half the number of chromosomes found in ordinary body cells. When the egg and sperm join, half the male chromosomes and half the female chromosomes combine to create a new individual. Since the female has only X chromosomes, she always contributes an X. But the male can contribute an X or a Y. An individual who inherits two X chromosomes will be a female. An individual who inherits an X and a Y will be male.

In 1905, Stevens published her findings about chromosomes, as did Edmund B. Wilson who by then had moved to Columbia University in New York City. At the time, both Stevens and Wilson were credited with independently making the same discovery about sex determination. However, over the years, Stevens's name tended to be dropped, and many people came to believe that Wilson alone had made the discovery. Science historians are now trying to correct this misunderstanding.

Nettie Marie Stevens's life was cut short just as her work was beginning to be recognized. After developing breast cancer in the early 1900s, she went to Johns Hopkins Hospital in Baltimore for treatment. Sadly, there was nothing they could do to save her and she died at the hospital on May 4, 1912.

Valentina V. Tereshkova

1937-
Cosmonaut

Russia's Valentina Tereshkova was determined to become a cosmonaut. Even though she had little higher education and was merely a technologist at a cotton factory, she was determined to achieve her goal. She joined an air sports club and became an expert at parachuting from planes. After cosmonaut Yuri A. Gagarin became the first man to fly in space, Tereshkova wrote to the Soviet space authorities and volunteered for the space program. To her great delight, she was accepted, and on June 16, 1963, Tereshkova became the first woman to fly in space.

Valentina Tereshkova was born on March 6, 1937, in a small village near Yaroslavl, a city on the Volga River northeast of Moscow in what was then the Soviet Union. When Valentina was a child, Russia was involved in World War II (1939-1945). In 1941, the armed forces of Nazi Germany and its allies invaded the Soviet Union, inflicting millions of casualties on the military personnel defending the country. Valentina's father, a tractor driver in civilian life, was one of the soldiers killed.

His death and the shortages caused by the war left Valentina, her mother, brother, and sister nearly destitute. Valentina did not even begin school until she was ten years old. At age seventeen, she became an apprentice at the local tire factory but continued to study at night school. Within a few months, she was given a position at the cotton mill where her mother and sister worked. She learned to operate a loom, took courses in cotton technology, and began parachuting with the Yaroslavl air sports club. She made more than 100 jumps.

At this time, parachuting ability was an important part of cosmonaut training. Cosmonauts reentering Earth's atmosphere were required to eject from their spacecraft and parachute to Earth. So Tereshkova's qualifications and love of the space program were sufficient to attract the attention of the Soviet space program directors. In 1962, she was called to Star City outside Moscow to begin training. She studied rocketry and spacecraft design. After nine months of training, she was given the military rank of junior lieutenant.

The Soviet space program was wrapped in secrecy. This was the era of the Cold War between the United States and its Western allies and the Soviet Union and its Eastern satellite countries. In addition, the United States and the Soviet Union were locked in a vital space race, because both sides considered mastery of space to be of great military importance. Nevertheless, word leaked out that Tereshkova was undergoing training for space flight and that she displayed awesome physical stamina, such as exposure to fifteen times the force of gravity in a whirling centrifuge.

On June 16, 1963, Tereshkova squeezed into her *Vostok* 6 space capsule on the launch pad at Baikonur, Kazakhstan, and blasted off into space. While in orbit, she communicated with a cosmonaut orbiting Earth in another Soviet space capsule. She stayed aloft for 70 hours and 50 minutes before reentering Earth's atmosphere. At a height of more than four miles, she ejected from the craft and parachuted to the ground.

Tereshkova was an immediate hero and brought the Soviet Union to the attention of the world. She was honored with parades and the government's highest honor. At a huge rally in Moscow's Red Square, Premier Nikita Khrushchev presented Tereshkova as living proof that the West's notion of women being the weaker sex was unfounded. Nevertheless, it was not until 1982 that another Russian woman, Svetlana Savitskaya, went into space.

For several years after her historic flight, Valentina Tereshkova remained in the cosmonaut program. Eventually, she returned to more active participation in Communist Party activities and was elected to a seat on the powerful Central Committee. In November 1963, she married fellow cosmonaut Andrian Nikolayev. They have one daughter.

MARY WATSON WHITNEY

1847-1920
Astronomer

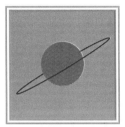

Mary Whitney was very good at math. All her teachers were impressed with how intelligent she was and how quickly she learned. But after high school, there was nowhere to go for further study. None of the colleges in the eastern United States accepted women students in the 1860s — not until Vassar College for Women opened its doors in September 1865 in Poughkeepsie, New York. Then Mary Whitney was there to enroll. Not only did she earn bachelor's and master's degrees at Vassar, but she eventually returned as an astronomy professor and as the second director of Vassar's astronomical observatory. Under her guidance and expertise, the first generation of highly trained women astronomers were educated.

Mary Watson Whitney was born on September 11, 1847, in Waltham, Massachusetts, the second of five children. Her parents, Samuel and Mary Watson Whitney, came from a long line of colonial Americans, the first of whom came to New England in 1635. Mary's parents had progressive ideas for the times and believed in providing for the education of all their children — boys and girls alike.

Mary Whitney proved to be a very capable and popular student. She served as an officer of various student organizations and became a favorite pupil of the first great American woman astronomer, Maria Mitchell, who was a professor at Vassar and director of the observatory. Whitney majored in astronomy and graduated in 1868. In 1872, Vassar College awarded her a master's degree. Then from 1874 to 1876, she studied mathematics in Switzerland, where her sister was attending medical school. Despite Mary Whitney's education and remarkable achievements, the only employment open to her when she returned home was as a teacher at Waltham High School.

In 1881, Whitney's career outlook began to brighten. Maria Mitchell hired Whitney as her personal assistant. At Vassar, Whitney built her reputation as a fine teacher and an excellent astronomical observer. When Mitchell resigned in 1888, Whitney succeeded her as professor of astronomy and director of the Vassar College Observatory. She became a strong, active supporter of higher education for women. Although she added substantially to the bank of astronomical data and was a charter member of the American Astronomical Society, it is as an educator of women astronomers that she is chiefly remembered. Illness forced her to retire from Vassar in 1910, and she died on January 20, 1920. Just before she passed away, Mary Watson Whitney was reported to have said, "I hope when I get to Heaven I shall not find the women playing second fiddle."

CHIEN-SHIUNG WU

1912
Experimental Physicist

In 1936, after saying good-bye to her friends, her mother and father, and her two brothers, Chien-Shiung Wu sailed from Shanghai, China to the United States. She intended to get her Ph.D. in physics and then return to China, but she never saw her family again. World events intervened to change her life and the entire course of history. In 1937, Japan invaded eastern China. Two years later, Germany invaded Poland and allied itself with Japan. Succeeding military events precipitated World War II (1939-1945). After the war, a revolution led by Mao Tse-tung brought all of China under Communist control. As a result, Chien-Shiung Wu did not return to China until 1973. By then, all of her family and most of her friends had died, and she was known as the American physicist who had overturned one basic law of nature and confirmed another.

Chien-Shiung Wu was born in Liu ho, a town about thirty miles from Shanghai. Her mother was a schoolteacher, and her father owned and operated the first school for girls in their region. China, which was still ruled by regional warlords in some areas, was struggling with ideas of nationalism and modernization. Western ideas of democracy and women's rights were only beginning to penetrate Chinese society. At that time, some parents still practiced the tradition of binding their daughters' feet — a practice that stunted the growth of girls' feet, keeping the feet unnaturally small and making walking almost impossible.

Wu's parents, however, believed in new ideas, especially in the education of women. Disregarding standards, they enrolled her in a school they had started, which then only went through the fourth grade. In 1922, Wu transferred to a boarding school in Suzhou, near Shanghai. After graduating at the top of her class in 1930, she was accepted at the prestigious National Central University in Nanjing.

This was a time of great unrest in China. Fearing a Japanese invasion, a nationalist student movement arose in China to support their President Chiang Kai-shek in his efforts to oppose a takeover. As one of the student leaders at National Central University, Wu helped organize a boycott of Japanese goods and led a nationalist demonstration at the Presidential Mansion in Nanjing, where she spoke with Chiang Kai-shek and urged him to oppose Japanese aggression.

In 1936, Wu arrived in the United States, intending to enroll at the University of Michigan. But for a variety of reasons, she chose instead to attend the University of California at Berkeley. She had been at Berkeley about a year when news came that Japan had invaded China. With Shanghai and Nanjing under Japanese rule, there was no way she could return home. Cut off from her homeland and from her family's financial support, she felt stranded.

Wu was a brilliant student, so Berkeley's physics department took care of her housing and tuition. She took comfort and inspiration from the example of French nuclear physicist Marie Curie, who also had been exiled from her homeland because of war. Like Madame Curie, Wu worked long hours in her laboratory.

In 1940, Chien-Shiung Wu received her Ph.D. and became widely known as an expert on nuclear fission. In 1942, she married Luke Yuan, a Chinese physicist. They then moved to the east coast, where he worked on radar at Princeton, New Jersey, and she taught at Smith College in Massachusetts. They met on weekends in New York City. During World War II, Wu worked at Columbia University on the Manhattan Project to build the atom bomb. After the war, Wu stayed on as a research scientist at Columbia, and Yuan worked on building accelerators (atom smashers) at Brookhaven National Laboratory on Long Island, New York.

Much of Wu's research focused on a type of radioactivity called beta decay. This occurs when the atomic nucleus of one element changes into another element. It undergoes a transformation that involves a neutron turning into a proton with the emission of an electron and a neutrino. In 1933, Italian physicist Enrico Fermi had proposed that a nuclear force, called the weak interaction, was responsible for beta decay. According to Fermi's theory, the beta particle that flies out of the nucleus in this type of radioactive decay is a high-speed electron. But experimentation by physicists at that time had only been able to find slow-moving electrons resulting from beta decay.

To measure speeds of electrons, physicists exposed them to sheets of radioactive materials and calculated how long it took the electrons to pass through the sheets. When Wu analyzed these experiments, she found that even though these sheets were very thin, their thickness varied. As the electrons passed through the thicker sections, they slammed into and bounced off atoms. This is what slowed the electrons down. So Wu set up a series of precisely controlled experiments to study electrons passing through sheets of uniform thickness and found that they were traveling at high speeds just as Fermi had predicted.

Meanwhile, theorists were proposing theories of how the nucleus of an atom behaves. And they found that in many cases the world of the atom was not like that of the everyday world. In the everyday world, for example, a basic law of physics called the conservation of parity states that all objects and their mirror images behave the same way, but with the left hand and right hand reversed. For example, to uncork a bottle, a corkscrew is turned clockwise, or to the right. In a mirror image of this action, the corkscrew turns counterclockwise, or to the left. Two Chinese-American physicists in the 1950s saw evidence in particle accelerator experiments that caused them to question this. These men, Tsung Dao Lee and Chen Ning Yang, asked Wu to design an experiment that would answer the question: Was parity conserved in nuclear reactions involving the weak interaction?

Wu used beta rays to find out. She designed a complex and delicate experiment that called for chilling radioactive cobalt to 0.01 degree above absolute zero, -459° F. Near absolute zero, almost all atomic motion ceases. Heat and motion are closely related. And Wu needed to remove all motion that might interfere with her experimental results.

The experiment was conducted at the National Bureau of Standards in Washington, D.C., the only laboratory with adequate cooling equipment. The chilled radioactive cobalt was subject to a magnetic field that caused the spinning cobalt in nuclei to line up in the same direction. The scientists then waited for the nuclei to decay and in the process give off beta rays. Detectors counted the electrons ejected and the direction in which they flew. The results were clear. Rather than being ejected equally in opposite directions, the electrons had a preference for the direction opposite the direction of spin, like a left-handed corkscrew. The experiment proved that at least in the world of the atom, the law of parity had to be taken off the books.

For the discovery that the law of parity was not conserved, Lee and Yang won the 1957 Nobel Prize for Physics. To Wu's disappointment, she was not included. But she was given many other honors. Princeton University granted her its first honorary doctorate awarded to a woman. She was elected to the U.S. National Academy of Sciences and to the Academy of Science in China. She also was awarded the National Medal of Science and became a full professor at Columbia University, where she continued to conduct nuclear research and taught until her retirement in 1981.

Wu's third famous experiment confirmed the conservation of vector current, a law of physics proposed by Murray Gell-Mann, a theoretical physicist at the California Institute of Technology in Pasadena. Wu's experiment helped confirm that the weak force involved in beta decay is related to the electromagnetic force. Her work pointed toward the future of particle physics and the challenge facing the physicists of tomorrow: developing a theory that will unify the fundamental forces of nature — the strong force that holds the nucleus together, the weak force responsible for beta decay, the electromagnetic force that holds atoms together in molecules, and gravity that holds the planets, stars, and galaxies in place. This unification would define a master force that existed only at the moment of the universe's creation.

After her retirement, Chien-Shiung Wu lectured widely and encouraged the participation of young women in scientific careers.

ROSALYN YALOW

1921-
Medical Physicist

From the time she was a young girl, Rosalyn (Sussman) Yalow was very clear about what she wanted, and she always went after it in a determined, aggressive way. When she was in first grade, a teacher struck her with a ruler. She hit the teacher back. Later, in the principal's office, she explained that she had been waiting five years to avenge her older brother who had been struck by that same teacher. And as she grew older, Yalow realized that, as a Jewish woman trying to pursue a career in science in the 1940s, she would encounter discrimination in education and employment. But that did not bother her. Discrimination to her was just another obstacle to be conquered in her determined quest to have it all — marriage, children, and a brilliant scientific career. When Rosalyn Yalow finally had her own medical physics laboratory, she hung a sign in her office that said: "Whatever women do, they must do twice as well as men to be thought half as good. Luckily, this is not difficult." For helping to discover radioimmunoassay, a technique that is used to measure tiny quantities of biochemicals in the body, Yalow in 1977 became the first American-born woman to win the Nobel Prize for Physiology or Medicine.

Rosalyn Sussman was born on July 19, 1921, in the Bronx, New York. Her parents were European immigrants with no more than a grade-school education. They valued learning, but the family was very poor. So Rosalyn attended Hunter College, where the tuition was free. She decided on a physics career, because three good male physics teachers had taken her under their wing. After graduating from Hunter in 1941, Yalow accepted a position as a teaching assistant in the physics department at the University of Illinois in Urbana-Champaign. There she taught and worked on her doctorate, the only female faculty member among about 400 male colleagues.

In graduate school, she met Aaron Yalow, whom she married in 1943. They had two children — a son born in 1952 and a daughter in 1954. The new Mrs. Yalow assumed all the duties of running a household as well as attending to her graduate studies. She has always believed that shopping, cooking, and cleaning are the responsibilities of a wife, and that a woman has to work harder than a man.

The Yalows received their Ph.D.s in 1945 and returned to New York City. Aaron worked in medical physics at Montefiore Hospital, then became a professor of physics at Cooper Union. Rosalyn worked first as an electrical engineer at a telecommunications laboratory, then as a teacher at Hunter College. In time, her interest in nuclear physics, particularly radioisotopes, which are radioactive forms of chemical elements, led her into medicine. Because of Aaron's work at Montefiore, Rosalyn met the renowned medical physicist Edith Quimby, who put her in touch with people who could get her into the newly developing field. As a result, Rosalyn Yalow was hired as a consultant at the Bronx Veterans Administration Hospital. She continued teaching at Hunter College, however, until 1950.

Rosalyn Yalow joined the VA hospital's efforts to explore how radioisotopes could be used in medicine. The radioisotopes came from Oak Ridge and other national laboratories, which during World War II (1939-1945) had been producing radioactive material for the atomic bomb. It was not long before Solomon A. Berson, a resident physician, decided to join the department. In Berson, Yalow found the perfect collaborator for her work. She taught him physics and mathematics, he taught her anatomy and physiology. They proved to be one of the great teams of science, working 80-hour weeks and often staying up all night in the laboratory. They were so close that people often assumed they were husband and wife. Each, however, was happily married to another person.

Part of Yalow's and Berson's research procedure included "tagging" a biochemical, such as the hormone insulin, with a radioactive isotope, such as radioactive iodine. Afterward, they used radiation-detecting equipment to trace the biochemical. During the process of examining insulin levels, Yalow and Berson made an important discovery about the body's reaction to insulin treatment. They also discovered a powerful analytical tool that was to revolutionize medical research, especially the study of hormones.

Yalow and Berson were trying to determine whether all diabetics were deficient in insulin or whether some just could not use the insulin their bodies produced. They injected diabetic and nondiabetic volunteers with radio-tagged insulin, expecting the cells of the diabetics to take up the insulin more quickly. But just the opposite happened. The insulin stayed longer in the blood of diabetics. Yalow and Berson hypothesized that this occurred because the diabetics had developed antibodies to insulin. (Antibodies are molecules produced by the immune system to immobilize any foreign invader.) Because diabetics at the time were receiving insulin prepared from cows or pigs, Berson and Yalow assumed that the immune systems of the diabetics had been primed to produce antibodies against this insulin. So when the diabetic volunteers were injected, the antibodies immobilized some of the radio-tagged insulin.

The medical establishment at first rejected their conclusion, holding to the belief that insulin molecules were too small to stimulate antibody production. Refusing to be discouraged by the lack of support, Berson and Yalow continued, realizing that they could use antibodies

to analyze the tiniest quantities of insulin in the bloodstream. By placing radio-tagged and ordinary insulin in a test tube, they found that the two types competed to bind to the antibodies. The ratio of the tagged insulin to the untagged that bound to antibodies provided a measure of how much insulin there was in the sample. When there was a large amount of natural insulin, very little radioactive insulin could attach to the antibodies, and vice versa. Yalow and Berson then developed a scale of standards containing known amounts of insulin by which to compare unknown amounts.

After making this discovery in the late 1950s, they found they could use it to measure various hormones and other substances as well. So they set out, during the 1960s, to convince the scientific community of the value of this technique. They succeeded. Radioimmunoassay is now used in the diagnosis of such illnesses as diabetes, growth disorders, sexual dysfunction, and even some cancers. It is widely used to screen for underactive thyroid in newborns, once a major cause of mental retardation. It is used also to screen blood in blood banks for contaminants such as the hepatitis virus and to test individuals for drug abuse.

As the importance of radioimmunoassay grew, Yalow and Berson received numerous awards and honors. Although they both dreamed of winning the Nobel Prize one day, any hope of that seemed to end in April 1972, when Berson died suddenly of a heart attack. Yalow was personally devastated by the loss of her long-time research partner, but she never gave up. She found a new collaborator, named her laboratory at the VA hospital the Solomon A. Berson Research Laboratory, and continued her work.

In 1976, Rosalyn Yalow became the first woman to win the prestigious Albert Lasker Basic Medical Research Award. Then, in 1977, she received a call from Sweden announcing that she had won the Nobel Prize for Physiology or Medicine. Yalow retired officially from the VA in 1992 but remained there with a part-time secretary. Today, she continues to interact with the hospital as well as travel and lecture on the exaggerated fears of radioactivity at any level and also on the expanding role of women in science.

WOMEN INVENTORS AND ENGINEERS

Engineering was — and is — perhaps the most difficult science-related field for women to enter. And women have never been thought of as gifted inventors. Yet women have made important contributions to some of the greatest engineering triumphs of modern times — from the Brooklyn Bridge to the design of efficient manufacturing methods. Women have also come up with some less revolutionary inventions — such as typing correction fluid — that nevertheless have made everyday tasks easier or more convenient.

One of the best known women in technology was industrial engineer and psychologist Lillian Moller Gilbreth (1878-1972). She and her husband Frank, whom she married in 1904, developed the technique of time and motion studies. They observed and filmed workers on the job, trying to determine the one best way to do a task — the one that would require the least amount of effort. They began this work at Frank Gilbreth's construction company, then became consultants to other factory owners. Lillian Gilbreth later introduced the human factor into the design of manufacturing systems, taking into consideration the feelings and motivations of the workers.

Frank died in 1924, leaving Lillian to raise their twelve children. After his death, many firms canceled their consulting contracts because they did not think she could handle the task. But Lillian Gilbreth went on to gain fame at Purdue University as a professor of management, a lecturer, and an author. Her book, *Psychology of Management*, published in 1914, was a classic text for scientific management. She also applied her industrial management techniques to home economics and to the creation of devices and techniques to improve the lives of people with disabilities. She even designed a model kitchen for handicapped persons. Two of her children immortalized her in the humorous memoir, *Cheaper By the Dozen.*

While Lillian Gilbreth was helping to invent industrial engineering, Edith Clarke (1883-1959) was making important contributions to the field of electrical engineering. Working for the General Electric Company, she analyzed problems involving power transmission and simplified the calculation of power transmission line performance. She also racked up an impressive list of firsts: The first woman to receive a master's degree in electrical engineering from the Massachusetts Institute of Technology, the first woman to teach electrical engineering at a U.S. university (University of Texas), and the first woman fellow of what is now the Institute of Electrical and Electronics Engineers.

A woman was ultimately responsible for one of the greatest civil engineering feats of the late 1800s — construction of the Brooklyn Bridge in New York City. Emily Roebling was the wife of Washington Augustus Roebling, charged with carrying out construction of the suspension bridge his father designed. But during the construction project, Washington became an invalid — paralyzed, partially blind, deaf, and mute. Only Emily could communicate with him. So it was she who spent years on the site directing construction of what was the longest suspension bridge in the world when it was completed in 1883.

Another woman involved in a project solely credited to a man was Katherine Greene, who with the manager of her Mulberry Grove plantation, charged Eli Whitney with the task of inventing the cotton gin. Historians still debate her role, and the answer may never be known. But in the mid-1800s, stories began to circulate that it was she who suggested to Whitney that he use wire rather than wooden teeth to comb the seeds from cotton.

There are thousands of inventions we know were made by women, because they are registered in the U.S. patent office. These range from ingenious household items to designs for locomotives and flying machines. Some women made fortunes from their inventions. One of the most famous of these was Bette Nesmith Graham (1924-1980), who invented Liquid Paper for whiting out typing errors when she was working at a Texas bank as a secretary with very poor typing skills. She and her son developed the business, then in 1979, she sold Liquid Paper to the Gillette Company for more than $47 million.

Other products with household names were invented by women. Scotchgard fabric protector was co-invented by Patsy O. Sherman, a research chemist at the 3M Company. Kevlar, a high-strength fiber used in many products from radial tires to spacecraft, was invented by DuPont polymer chemist Stephanie L. Kwolek.

Women are still on the technical frontier. One of the advances that engineers predict the world can look forward to is superconductivity, the flow of electricity without resistance. Superconducting transmission lines could carry electric power for thousands of miles and superconducting magnets could float fleets of high speed trains just above the ground. Solid-state physicist and electrical engineer Mildred Dresselhaus, professor of engineering and physics and former director of M.I.T.'s Center for Materials Science and Engineering, has contributed to the technology that might make this possible .

Although their numbers are still relatively small, more young women are now choosing to study engineering. And in university and industry laboratories today, women inventors and engineers are working on technologies that will change our lives tomorrow.

BIBLIOGRAPHY

American Men and Women of Science, 1992-93. R. R. Bowker, 1992.

Bakker, Robert T. "Unearthing the Jurassic," *Science Year*, 1995.

Bataille, Gretchen M. (ed.). *Native American Women*. Garland Publishing, 1993.

Bendiner, Jessica, and Elmer Bendiner. *Biographical Dictionary of Medicine*. Facts On File, 1990.

Bateson, Katherine. *With a Daughter's Eye*. W. Morrow, 1984.

Benedict, Ruth. *Patterns of Culture*. Houghton Mifflin, 1934.

Briggs, Carol S. *Women in Space*. Lerner, 1988.

Brooks, Paul. *The House of Life: Rachel Carson at Work*. Houghton Mifflin, 1972.

Cambridge Biographical Dictionary. Cambridge University Press, 1990.

Carson, Rachel. *The Sea Around Us*. Oxford University Press, 1951.

Carson, Rachel. *The Edge of the Sea*. Houghton Mifflin, 1955.

Carson, Rachel. *Silent Spring*. Houghton Mifflin, 1962.

Crawford, Deborah. *Lise Meitner, Atomic Pioneer*. Crown Publishers, 1969.

Curie, Eve. *Madame Curie*. Doubleday, 1937.

Curie, Marie. *Pierre Curie*. Macmillan, 1923.

Dictionary of American Biography. Charles Scribner's Sons, 1974.

Dictionary of National Biography. The Concise Dictionary, Oxford University Press, 1953.

Dictionary of Scientific Biography. Charles Scribner's Sons, 1972.

Farber, Eduard. *Nobel Prize Winners in Chemistry (1901-1961)*. Abelard-Schuman, 1963.

Fossey, Dian. *Gorillas in the Mist*. Houghton Mifflin, 1983.

Gleasner, Diana C. *Breakthrough: Women in Science*. Walker, 1983.

Goodall, Jane. *My Friends, the Wild Chimpanzees*. Washington, National Geographic Society, 1967.

Goodall, Jane. *My Life with the Chimpanzees*. Pocket Books, 1988.

Goodall, Jane. *The Chimpanzees of Gombe: Patterns of Behavior*. Belknap Press of Harvard University Press, 1986.

Goodall, Jane. *Through a Window: My Thirty Years with the Chimpanzees*. Houghton Mifflin, 1990.

Haber, Louis. *Women Pioneers of Science*. 1979.

James, Edward T. (ed.). *Notable American Women: 1607-1950*. Belknap Press of Harvard University Press, 1971.

Jezer, M. *Rachel Carson*. Chelsea House, 1988.

Judson, H. F. *The Eighth Day of Creation*. Simon and Schuster, 1979.

Kass-Simon. *Women of Science: Righting the Record*. Indiana University Press, 1990.

Keller, Evelyn Fox. *A Feeling for the Organism: The Life and Work of Barbara McClintock*. W. H. Freeman, 1983.

Leakey, Mary. *Disclosing the Past*. Doubleday, 1984.

Levi-Montalcini, Rita. *In Praise of Imperfection: My Life and Work*. 1988.

McHenry, Robert (ed). *Famous American Women*. Dover, 1983.

McGrayne, Sharon Bertsch. *Nobel Prize Women of Science*. Birch Lane Press, 1993.

McGraw-Hill Encyclopedia of World Biography. 1973.

McLenighan, Valjean. *Women and Science*. Raintree, 1979.

Mead, Margaret. *And Keep Your Powder Dry: An Anthropologist Looks at America*. W. Morrow, 1942, 1965.

Mead, Margaret. *Coming of Age in Samoa*. W. Morrow, 1928, 1961.

Mead, Margaret. *Growing Up in New Guinea*. W. Morrow, 1930.

Modern Scientists and Engineers. McGraw-Hill, 1980.

Noble, Iris. *Contemporary Women Scientists of America*. Messner, 1979.

Notable American Women. 1607-1950. Harvard/Belknap Press, 1971.

Ogilvie, Marilyn Baily. *Women in Science*. MIT Press, 1986.

O'Hern, Elizabeth. *Profiles of Pioneer Women Scientists*. Acropolis Books, 1985.

Opfell, Olga S. *The Lady Laureates: Women Who Have Won the Nobel Prize*. Scarecrow Press, 1986.

Pflaum, Rosalynd. *Grand Obsession: Madame Curie and Her World*. Doubleday, 1989.

Reid, Robert. *Marie Curie*. E.P. Dutton, 1974.

Riedman, Sarah R. and Elton T. Gustafson. *Portraits of Nobel Laureates in Medicine and Physiology*. Abelard-Schuman, 1963.

Rossiter, Margaret. *Women Scientists in America: Struggles and Strategies to 1940*. Johns Hopkins University Press, 1982.

Schlessinger, Bernard S. and June H. Schlessinger. *The Who's Who of Nobel Prize Winners 1901-1990*. Oryx Press, 1991.

Science Is Women's Work. National Women's History Project, 1993.

Sicherman, Barbara and Carol Hurd Green, (eds.). *Notable American Women: The Modern Period*. Belknap Harvard Press, 1980.

Sayre, Anne. *Rosalind Franklin and DNA*. W. W. Norton, 1975.

Smith, Jessey Carney (ed.). *Notable Black American Women*. Gale, 1992.

Stoddard, Hope. *Famous American Women*. Crowell, 1970.

Veglahn, Nancy J. *Women Scientists*. Facts on File, 1991.

Watson, James. *The Double Helix*. Atheneum, 1968.

Weber, Robert L. *Pioneers of Science: Nobel Prize Winners in Physics*. Institute of Physics, 1980.

Williams, Trevor I. *A Biographical Dictionary of Scientists*. Wiley Interscience, 1982.

Yost, Edna. *Women of Modern Science*. Dodd Mead, 1962.

INDEX

PHOTO ACKNOWLEDGMENTS

Cover, 1, 3, Bryn Mawr College Archives; 10-15, The Bettmann Archive; 17, The Natural History Museum, London; 19, 21, 22, Smith College Archives, Smith College; 26, Courtesy of the Open University; 30, Courtesy of Columbia University; 33, Harvard College Observatory; 34, 36, UPI/Bettmann; 37, Mount Holyoke College Archives; 39, The Bettmann Archive; 40, Rachel Carson History Project © Shirley A. Briggs; 43, Courtesy of Dr. Jewel P. Cobb; 46, AP/Wide World Photos; 49, UPI/Bettmann; 51, 54, The Bettmann Archive; 57, Courtesy of The Dakota Indian Foundation; 59, Special Collections, California Academy of Science; 62, Museum of Comparative Zoology, Harvard University; 66, Courtesy of Burroughs Wellcome Co.; 69, Harvard College Observatory; 71, 73, AP/Wide World Photos; 76, Courtesy of Professor R. G. Gosling; 79, UPI/Bettmann; 81, Photo by Ken Regan/HBO Courtesy of the Jane Goodall Institute, PO Box 599, Ridgefield, CT 06877; 84, Smith College Archives, Smith College; 86, UPI/Bettmann; 87, 89, AP/Wide World Photos; 92, UPI/Bettmann; 95, Kansas University Archives; 98, NASA; 99, UPI/Bettmann; 105, The Bettmann Archive; 107, 110, 112, UPI/Bettmann; 114, Harvard College Observatory; 118, Courtesy of Washington University in St. Louis; 121, Harvard College Observatory; 125, 131, 135, AP/Wide World Photos; 136, 139, 142, UPI/Bettmann; 146, The Bettmann Archive; 147, Vassar College Library; 153, NASA; 155, AP/Wide World Photos; 159, UPI/Bettmann; 161, Photograph by Stanford University Medical Photography, Stanford, California; 163, NASA; 164, UPI/Bettmann; 167, The MIT Museum; 170, 171, NASA; 175, Carnegie Institution of Washington; 178, Smith College Archives, Smith College; 182, Bryn Mawr College Archives; 185, UPI/Bettmann; 187, Vassar College Library; 189, 194, UPI/Bettmann
Original illustrations © Lindaanne Donohoe Design

ABOUT THE AUTHOR

Darlene R. Stille is a Chicago-based science writer and editor. Currently the managing editor of the *World Book Annuals*, Ms. Stille has traveled throughout the world, from the rainforests of Costa Rica and Thailand to the mountains of Tibet and along China's Yangtze River.

She has an extensive background in the sciences, first as a premed student and then as a science editor for more than twenty-five years. Books she has written for Childrens Press include *Air Pollution*, *The Greenhouse Effect*, *Oil Spills*, *The Ozone Hole*, *Soil Erosion and Pollution*, and *Water Pollution*.

Ms. Stille belongs to the National Association of Science Writers and the American Association for the Advancement of Science. She helped found Women Employed, an organization devoted to the equal employment of women, and was the first chairwoman of this Chicago-based organization from 1973 to 1976.

ABOUT THE DESIGNER–ILLUSTRATOR

Lindaanne Yee-Donohoe is a freelance designer and illustrator, working in both advertising design and educational publishing. For Childrens Press she has designed and electronically produced several popular series: *Encyclopedia of Presidents*, *The World's Great Explorers*, and *Extraordinary People*.

Ms. Yee-Donohoe's design of *Extraordinary Women Scientists*, the fifth book of the series, expresses both the ethereal and substantive nature of women in science as they struggled to perform their roles as daughters, wives, mothers, and educated women excelling in a male-dominated world. She has combined passionate purple tones (representing commitment and dedication to work) and brown earthy colors (symbolizing key areas of science — matter and energy) with warm yellows and a brilliant gold (indicating awards for outstanding achievement).